S. CONNOLLY
S. AMANDA
& ADDITIONAL CONTRIBUTORS

THE KITCHEN WITCH COOKBOOK

40+ AMAZING RECIPES TO BRING MORE MAGIC INTO YOUR LIFE

The Kitchen Witch Cookbook
Darkerwood Publishing Group LLC, Denver, CO

Available In:
eBook
Paperback
Case Wrap Hardcover
Linen Wrap Hardcover
Spiral Bound

Editorial: Connie Bauldree and M. Blackthorne
Cover: S. Connolly
Interior Design by Connie Bauldree, Author by Design

DB Publishing
An Imprint of Darkerwood Publishing Group LLC

The table of

CONTENTS

Continuation of the table of

CONTENTS

OUR CONCEPT

KITCHEN WITCH COOKBOOK

The Kitchen Witch Cookbook is more than just a collection of recipes—it's a magical guide to transforming everyday meals into rituals of nourishment and empowerment. Each of the 40 recipes is carefully crafted to infuse intention and meaning into the kitchen, inviting you to connect with your inner magic. Whether you're looking to stir love into your morning tea, bake protection into your bread, or create an energy-boosting potion, this cookbook is your guide. At the heart of kitchen witchery lies the belief that cooking is an alchemical process, where simple ingredients can be transformed into something truly powerful.

The Kitchen Witch Cookbook teaches you how to harness this magic by using food as a tool for manifestation, healing, and celebration. From understanding the energy of herbs and spices to learning how to infuse your dishes with positive intentions, each recipe offers a journey into the world of culinary magic. Through this book, you'll discover how to elevate your daily meals into moments of enchantment, where cooking becomes an act of love, creativity, and spiritual connection.

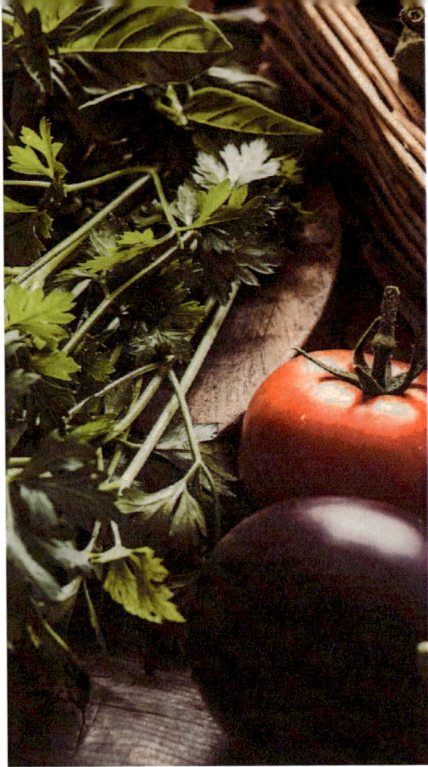

INTRODUCTION
KITCHEN WITCH COOKBOOK

I am unashamedly a kitchen witch. I mix well wishes into cakes, and healing into pot roast. I mix calming teas with calming energy. I pick ingredients based on their magical properties. The best part is, I'm not alone. Thousands of witches the world over have turned their kitchens into magical havens and imbue their meals with magical intent. Over the past few years, I've picked up books about kitchen witchery. Imagine my sadness and dismay when I realized almost none of them, minus one book, had any real recipes imbued with witchy spells and intent. This confounded me since any good kitchen witch worth her salt, is also worth her sage, rosemary, thyme, cayenne, and a great dish or two.

So, I set out to find a whole host of witchy recipes from people of all paths and traditions to put together an honest to goodness magical cookbook with not just teas and elixirs in it, but actual FOOD recipes you can make in order to manifest your will. Joining me in this search is S. Amanda, who is an amazing cook and witch whose Southern recipes are to die for.

You won't find the basics of witchcraft in this book. You'll need to look elsewhere for that. See the resources section at the back of the book. But we have included how to imbue your food with magical intent, magical food correspondence charts, magical herb correspondence charts, plenty of recipes from bread and appetizers to soups and stews, main dishes, and deserts, to teas and drinks.

We've also included some basic cooking information, like how to adjust your recipe for high altitude, how to substitute items you don't have, what temperatures meat should be at to be safe, and conversion charts. All the things beginner and intermediate cooks alike might want in a cookbook. Even if you're not a witch, try some of these recipes and see what manifests! Happy cooking and we hope you enjoy these recipes.

~ S. Connolly, Autumn/Winter 2024

MAGICAL HOW-TO

KITCHEN WITCH COOKBOOK

Since some of you picking up this book may be absolutely new to the practice of witchcraft, we thought we'd include a section giving some basics of magic to help you get started. To see all the measurement tables, substitutions, and lists of food and their magical uses, see the back of the book.

Cleansing and Consecrating your Kitchen and Kitchen Tools:

Cleansing and consecrating your kitchen and kitchen tools can be as simple or as elaborate as you wish. Some witches just use a little dishwashing liquid, some elbow grease, and a statement of intent such as, "I cleanse and consecrate this [name of kitchen tool] with the power of magic so that my will is done. So be it."

Some witches might burn sage or rosemary and fumigate the kitchen to remove negativity. Others might simply say a blessing over each tool before they put it back in the cupboard after running it through the dishwasher. Some witches may not bother with this step at all because they love being in the kitchen and nourishing others, and that intent builds up in their kitchen tools as they use them.

Your kitchen is your own, and how you cleanse and consecrate your utensils, dishes, pots and pans is entirely up to you.

Imbuing Food with Intent:

Imbuing food with intent does require being able to concentrate on your intent as you prepare and mix the ingredients and as you cook and add spices. Visualize a blue, healing light around your loved ones while you whip up a healing stew. Or visualize your annoying coworker leaving the company after you give her that cake you made just for her. Regardless which spell you're infusing into the recipe, be sure to visualize the outcome you want in a way that makes sense to you. Most of the time, you'll be using your kitchen witch powers for good, but when using them to remove unwanted people or situations, be sure to be specific and do your best to not include anyone or any situation in that visualization that you don't want to drive away.

That way, recipes meant to rid yourself of unwanted people or situations won't harm the wrong target and will be rendered inert for anyone else also eating the dish. Remember, with magic – intent is everything.

You may also want to ground yourself and clear your head of any negative thoughts before you begin cooking so that you don't accidentally mix your own negativity into any food that you serve. Always enter the kitchen with a calm and focused head.

Gods and Goddesses for the Kitchen Witch

Not all kitchen witches are pagan, but many pagans and pagan-type religions have witchy and magical practices that extend into the kitchen. In various cultural pantheons of gods and goddesses, there are those deities who rule over food.

In Hindu mythology, there is the goddess Annapurna, who is a manifestation of the goddess of Parvati and daughter of the god of the mountains, Himavat. Annapurna is the goddess of food, nourishment, and abundance.

In Greek mythology you have Dionysus, who was a god of wine, feasting, and celebration. There was also Hestia, the goddess of hearth, home, and family, who ruled over the preparation and sharing of meals within households. Then, perhaps a bit further removed, you have Hermes, who - while he was a messenger god, he also was said to influence food markets and exchanges.

In Roman mythology, there was Ceres (Demeter in Greek mythology) who was the goddess of agriculture, fertility and grains.

These are merely a few of the many pagan gods and goddesses who ruled over food.

Additional food related gods and goddesses include Hathor (Egypt), Cernunnos (Celtic), and Xochipilli (Aztec) who were gods of agriculture or the harvest.

As a kitchen witch you are not required to work with gods or goddesses, but if you happen to be pagan, we thought this little list might inspire you in ways you can work magic and spirituality into your magical food preparation.

Tasty Breads

Bread is the foundation of sustenance, kneaded with intention and baked with care. In every loaf lies the magic of warmth, comfort, and connection.

Squash Bread
by Annette Archambeau

INGREDIENTS

1 (.25oz) package	**Dry Yeast**
2 tbsp	**Warm Water (add yeast and set aside)**
1 cup	**Mashed-pureed cooked sqaush (Butternut or Big Ole Squash)**
1/3 cup	**Warm Milk (110-115 Degrees F)**
1/4 cup	**Melted Butter**
1 egg	**Egg (Room Temperature)**
3 tbsp	**Raw Honey (locally sourced is best)**
1/4 tsp	**Salt**
3 cups	**Flour (I use non-gmo, Montana Wheat, White Flour)**
2 tbsp	**Powdered Pumpkin Seed**
2 tbsp	**Powdered Maca Root**
	GLAZE:
1	**Egg beaten**
1 tbsp	**Water**

THE GIFT OF THE SQUASH BREAD

This bread is meant to be shared with a community. It can also be used to share during group or individual ritual, and/or it can be used as an offering to the spirits. The following prayer goes with the squash bread, and you may say it before you begin the dish, during the mixing stage, and/or after it is baked. This will seal in the intent:

The Gift of The Squash Bread
We honor and call upon the energy of the Sun, Sol.
We gather the vitality, warmth and illumination baked into this bread, a storage place of the Sun's ultimate energy. Allow us to share your energies of abundance, health and protection, as individuals and as a group.

DIRECTIONS

Add the flour gradually to the wet ingredients. The dough should be sticky. I knead my bread in the mixing bowl, add flour to coat the bowl and continue to mix the flour into dough until a smooth and elastic texture is achieved. This translates to about 5-10 minutes of kneading.

Cover the dough in the bowl with a tea towel, and let it rise to double its original size in a warm place. 1-2 hours.

Next, form the dough into rolls or loafs. Place them on ungreased cookie sheets or in a greased loaf pan. You can divide the dough into 3 portions, form rolled ropes, and braid together, as another option, to create a beautiful, braided loaf.

Let the bread rise again, until double, which can take 30 minutes to an hour.
Mix the glaze together and brush over the bread just before baking.

Bake at 350 for 20-25 minutes for a loaf, or 15 minutes for the rolls. Adjust for altitude or just check it and take it out once the crust is golden brown.

SERVING	TIME	KCAL.	LEVEL
20	3-4 hours	145 approx. per serving	intermediate

Fertile Myrtle Southern Skillet Cornbread

by S. Amanda

LEVEL
easy

KCAL.
179
approx. per serving

TIME
60
mins

SERVING
6

INGREDIENTS

1 Cup	**Cornmeal**
1/2 cup	**Flour**
1 tbsp	**Baking Powder**
1/2 tsp	**Baking Soda**
1 tsp	**Solar Charged Sea Salt**
1	**Large Egg**
1 cup	**Buttermilk**
1/2 cup	**Whole milk**
1/4 cup	**Oil or Plain Lard (If using oil, vegetable is best - olive oil will not work well here)**
2 tbsp	**Lard, oil, or bacon grease for the skillet before you put the batter in to prevent sticking.**

DIRECTIONS

Preheat the oven to 400F. Paint the sigil of your choosing on the bottom of the skillet with some of the bacon grease or lard with your finger. You can use a daemon sigil of your choice, Unsere is great for fertility if you are having trouble choosing. I also like to create my own sigil in tandem with the daemon sigil. Then add the remaining 2 tbsp of grease to the bottom of the skillet; set aside.

In a large bowl, mix togother all dry ingredients with a wooden spoon. At this point, you can add an extra kick to your spell and draw a fertility symbol in the powder mix; set aside.

In a separate bowl, lightly whisk together the milk and buttermilk. Gently blow on the egg to give it warmth of life and your energies. Then whisk it into the milk. I prefer to use a silver fork or a wooden fork for whisking. Old silver, especially from an older generation, carries deep rooted maternal powers. I use my grandmother's silver to whisk for recipes like this.

Pour the wet ingredients into the dry - directly in the middle - to represent the egg and the womb coming together in perfect balance. Mix together with a wooden spoon roughly 12 times to represent the female moon cycles. There are generally 12 full moons each year - double check your calendar to determine how many full moons there will be before you do this and adjust accordingly. The mix will be lumpy, Set it aside for 12 to 13 minutes (dependent upon the number of moons). While that is sitting, put the skillet you set aside into the already preheated oven. Cover and let the grease melt.

When the batter has sat for the full 12 to 13 minutes, pour it into the preheated skillet in the oven.

Bake for about 40 minutes or until a toothpick inserted in the middle comes out clean and the top is a golden brown.

Remove from the oven and serve warm (about 20 minutes cool time). Add butter and a little extra buttermilk if you desire.

Know Thyself Breakfast Biscuit Spell
by S. Amanda

DIRECTIONS

Preheat the oven to 450F.

In a large bowl, draw a sigil of intent, sigil of the daemon, or spirit of your choosing. Buer is great for this as is Lucifer for gaining knowledge of the self. Lucifer also rules over logical thinking. Though you are welcome to work with your patron or matron god/goddess/spirit for this.

Next, whisk together the dry ingredients, including herbs. Speak your intentions into the ingredients as you stir.

Add butter or shortening in approximately 1 tbsp size chunks. I like to use both butter and shortening and work them into the dry mixture with my fingertips until the dough is crumbly and the consistency of damp sand.

Add the shredded cheese, tossing it with your hands to gently incorporate it into the mixture.

Next, create a well in the center of the dough and pour in the buttermilk. You can mix it with a wooden spoon, however, I prefer my hands for this because I can add more energies to the recipe this way. Mix until everything is moistened, but still crumbly.

Put the dough onto a floured surface and knead until it's smooth and comes together nicely. Don't overwork the dough or the biscuits will be tough to the palette and can make your spell's manifestation hit a bit harder. You want the results of the spell to come to fruition effortlessly and be easy to digest physically as well as magically.

Shape the dough into a flat square with your fingers - about a half an inch to an inch thick. Use a biscuit cutter, pizza cutter, or a drinking glass to cut out the biscuits.

Place the biscuits into an ungreased cast iron skillet, baking dish or cookie sheet. The dough can touch, but make sure it's not overlapping.

Brush the dough with melted butter and then place in the oven.

Bake for approximately 13 minutes which adds some extra luck to your spell, or until the biscuits are golden brown.

Once they're done, brush them with more melted butter and serve them with a tea of your choice and a little jam. Blueberry, raspberry, or apple jams/jellies are great for self-knowledge.

"Use herbs for cleansing, purifying, clearing, and unblocking the pathway of the mind. This will allow you to open up psychic abilities and gain knowledge."

KCAL.
232
approx. per serving

LEVEL
easy

SERVING
6

TIME
35
mins

INGREDIENTS

2 cups	**Self-rising flour**
6 tbsp	**Shortening or butter**
1/2 tsp	**Solar charged sea salt**
1/2 tsp	**Sugar**
1 cup	**Buttermilk**
4 tbsp	**Butter for later**
1 cup	**Shredded cheese**
1/4 tsp	**Nettle**
1/4 tsp	**Dandelion leaf**
1/4 tsp	**Rosemary**
1/4 tsp	**Thyme**
1/4 tsp	**Sage**
1/4 tsp	**Chicory (powder root or leaf)**
1/4 tsp	**Lemon balm**
1/4 tsp	**Mugwort**

Comfort & Joy White Bread (Perfect White Bread)

by S. Connolly

My mom used to make this white bread recipe, and we all loved it. Everytime she made it, a sense of comfort and joy radiated through the house because that's the energy she put into it. Which goes to prove that whatever energy you put into your cooking or baking, it manifests in those you share the food with.

You can do this in a bowl and hand knead, or you can use your mixer or bread machine. I'll give the instructions separately

SERVING	*TIME*	*KCAL.*	*LEVEL*
32	3.5 – 4 *hours*	107 *approx. per serving*	*easy*

INGREDIENTS

.25 oz	**1 package of active dry yeast**
1/4 *cup*	**Water heated to 110 degrees F**
2 cups	**Milk heated to 110 degrees F**
2 tbsp	**Sugar**
2 tsp	**Salt**
2 tbsp	**Shortening or butter**
5 3/4 to 6 1/4 cups	**White flour (you can substitute the flour for wheat or whole grain, just add an additional 2 tablespoons of butter so it's not as dry)**

DIRECTIONS

Set your intention to bring comfort and joy to your household or whomever you're making the bread for.

In a bowl – mix the water and yeast. Add the milk, sugar, salt and butter.

Then add 5 ¾ cup of flour – adding more as needed. Mix together until you have a relatively stiff, but pliable dough. Knead on a floured board until satiny and smooth (about 8-10 minutes). Shape into a ball and put it in a lightly greased bowl. Cover it with a tea towel and place the bowl in a warm place for an hour to an hour and fifteen minutes.

The dough will double. Punch the dough down and then divide the dough evenly into two balls. Put them into two lightly greased bread loaf pans, cover again, and let rise for another hour, up to an hour and fifteen minutes.

Bake in a preheated, 400F oven for 30-35 minutes or until done. Remember that at higher altitudes, things bake a little faster, so keep an eye on the bread.

Once done, remove from the oven and let the loaves cool in the loaf pans on top of a wire rack for 5-10 minutes, and then carefully flip the loaf pans over and the bread should release evenly. Let both loaves cool on the wire rack, covered, for an additional 20 minutes before eating or putting them in a plastic bag or container to preserve freshness.

Bread machine: In the bread machine, only heat the milk and water to 85F, add everything to the bread machine, then set your machine to the DOUGH setting. When finished, transfer the dough to two greased loaf pans and put into a preheated, 400F oven for 30-35 minutes or until done. (Basically, you don't do the second rise in the loaf pans for this one since the second rise will happen in the bread machine.)

Stand Mixer: The recipe remains the same for hand mixing except you would turn the mixer on medium/low to medium for 8-10 minutes until you have a stiff, but pliable dough. You can leave the dough in the mixer bowl, covered, to rise for an hour, then transfer to the loaf pans, cover for another hour to let it rise again. Then bake as above.

Sweetness is a spell all its own—baked with love, magic, and just a pinch of sugar, every bite brings joy to the soul.

CAKES, COOKIES, AND DESSERTS

SERVING	TIME	KCAL.	LEVEL
8	70 *mins*	330 *approx. per serving*	*easy*

Honey Jar Cake
by J. Priestly

DIRECTIONS

The name says it all, a honey jar in a cake. Bake and eat this cake to draw positive energies, manifest something you want or to sweeten any situation. The cake has cinnamon, honey and orange zest to attract positivity and/or prosperity.

Preheat the oven to 325F. Grease and flour a 9 inch round cake pan or line the bottom with parchment paper.

In a bowl, cream the butter,, sugar, and honey with a mixer until light and fluffy. Beat in eggs one at a time Mix in vanilla and orange zest.

In separate bowl, sift together flour, baking powder, baking soda, salt, and cinnamon.

Slowly mix the dry mixture into the wet mixture until just combined. Don't over mix.

Pour the batter into the prepared pan and smooth out.

Bake for about 40 minutes, until the cake tester inserted in the center comes out clean.

Sprinkle almonds on top after 20 minutes so they don't burn. Allow to cool and remove from the pan.

While preparing and mixing ingredients, speak or envision your intent and push that energy into the batter. While the cake bakes, envision the scent of the cake baking, filling and infusing your home with its energy. While you eat the cake, envision that your intent has already come to be.

INGREDIENTS

1/2 pound	**Unsalted butter (2 sticks) at room temperature**
1/2 cup	**Packed brown sugar**
1/3 cup	**Honey**
1 tsp	**Orange zest**
4	**Extra large eggs at room temperature**
1 tsp	**Vanilla**
1 cup	**All purpose flour**
1 tsp.	**Baking powder**
1/4 tsp	**Baking soda**
1/4 tsp	**Cinnamon**
1/2 tsp	**Kosher salt**
1/4 cup	**Sliced almonds (optional)**

19

Prosperity Bread Pudding

by J. C. DeCesari

INGREDIENTS

3	**Eggs**
1 1/4 cup	**Canned pumpkin**
1 cup	**Sugar**
1tsp	**Ginger**
1/2 tsp	**½ teaspoon nutmeg**
1/4 tsp	**Ground clove**
1 1/2 tsp	**Cinnamon**
12 oz can	**Evaporated milk**
1 cup	**Milk**
4 cups	**Day old bread, cubed (use cinnamon bread for extra kick)**
1/4 cup	**Red currants or golden raisins for garnish**
	Fresh whipped cream (I flavor mine with a dash of sugar and vanilla)

DIRECTIONS

Visualize prosperity while mixing up this delicious bread pudding.

In a large mixing bowl, beat the eggs, sugar, and spices together. Gradually beat in the pumpkin, evaporated milk, and milk. Add the bread cubes and mix together gently. Let the bread cubes soak for about 5 minutes.

Pour mixture into a 9 x 9 greased pan and sprinkle with the currants or raisins.

Bake in a preheated oven at 350F for 40 minutes or until a knife inserted into the center comes out clean. Serve warm or cold with the whipped cream.

SERVING	TIME	KCAL.	LEVEL
8	60 mins	261 approx. per serving	easy

Witch Cake

by Nathair Noxumbra

Make this cake as a gift to someone who may have been cursed or under a spell you know they would like to be free from. It can also protect from malevolent or unwanted witchcraft.

Ask your gatekeeper (daemonic, deitic etc) to open the way for the purpose of the cake. When some sort of accident or inconvenience occurs or you get that feeling under the back of your skull, proceed.

SERVING	TIME	KCAL.	LEVEL
10-12	2.5 hours	260 approx. per serving	easy

INGREDIENTS

1 tsp	**Cinnamon**
1 tsp	**Allspice**
1 tsp	**Ginger**
1/3 tsp	**Freshly ground nutmeg/mace**
1 Pinch	**Ground cloves**
1.5 tsp	**Salt**
1.5 tsp	**Baking soda**
1 cup	**Brown sugar**
2/3 cup	**Honey**
2.5 cups	**Flour**
2/3 cup	**Extra Virgin Olive Oil**
6	**Brown eggs**
1.5 cups	**Milk**
	Water

DIRECTIONS

Preheat the oven to 300F.

Grease and flour a large cake pan or two loaf pans.

Put the cinnamon in the bowl and thank the spirits for opening the gate.

Add the rest of the spices, the flour, and the baking soda.

Make a well in the middle of the dry ingredients.

While adding the salt, call to your Mother of Life on Earth (who you feel bonded to, etc) and ask Her to cleanse and protect the person(s). Stir the ingredients well.

In a separate bowl, add in the sugar, honey and oil while thinking of your gatekeeper and life spirit. Cream together with a whisk or electric mixer until it is somewhat fluffy.

Add in the eggs slowly while thinking about friendship and family bonds. Blend well.

In a separate dish, add lemon juice to the milk so that it curdles.

Add sugar, oil, and the egg mixture to the dry ingredients and mix well. While still mixing, add the curdled milk.

Add enough water to make a somewhat thick but pourable batter and mix until well combined.

Cover the bowl and project energy of protection and freedom from affliction into the batter. You may also pass it through incense smoke if you like.

Let it rest for 20 mins then pour the mixture into the prepared pan(s). Bake for one hour. Test it and if it isn't done give it 15 more mins. Cool on a wire rack, then wrap it in reflective food foil or a layer of parchment paper then foil.

Give and serve with love and confidence in your power. When you give this, it is important that it is wrapped in foil - reflective side up. Mirrors with benevolent energy send negativity back to the sender.

Pineapple Friendship Cake

by S. Connolly

INGREDIENTS

3 cups	**Flour**
2 cups	**Sugar**
1 tsp	**Salt**
1 tsp	**Baking soda**
1 1/2 tsp	**Cinnamon**
4	**Eggs**
1 1/4 cup	**Oil**
20 oz can	**Crushed pineapple (or you can use fresh)**
1 1/4 cups	**Nuts of your choice (optional with respect to nut allergies)**

DIRECTIONS

Pineapple has long been touted as the fruit that brings friendship and good will, as well as love and attraction. It has also been associated with prosperity. So, as you can imagine, a pineapple cake also brings all the happy feelings that come along with these things. Make this cake for a party, and people will rave about it.

While visualizing friends – bring the intention to draw something positive (prosperity, love etc…) to the gathering through the cake. As you prepare the cake, let your intention run into the ingredients as you mix.

First, beat the eggs and add the oil. Next, add the pineapple and nuts. In another bowl, mix together the dry ingredients and slowly add them bit by bit to the wet mixture and stir carefully. Once mixed, pour the mixture into a lightly greased springform pan.

Bake at 325F degrees for 1.5 hours or until you insert a toothpick and it comes out clean. (You can add a teaspoon of vanilla if you're making this cake for love.)

SERVING	TIME	KCAL.	LEVEL
12	2 hours	363 approx. per serving	easy

SERVING	TIME	KCAL.	LEVEL
24	2 *hours*	180 *approx. per serving*	*easy*

Magic Cookie Bars to Ehance Personal Power
by S. Connolly

DIRECTIONS

While following the recipe, visualize confidence and personal power in the people who will be eating these. Visualize the kids playing well or winning the game, or your spouse getting the project.

Preheat the oven to 350F degrees.

In a 13 x 9 pan, melt the butter in the pan in the oven.

When it's melted, take it out and sprinkle the graham cracker crumbs over the butter.

Pour the milk evenly over the crumbs.

Top with the remaining ingredients and press down firmly.

Bake for 25 to 30 minutes or until lightly browned.

Cool the pan then place in the refrigerator for an hour.

Remove from the refrigerator and cut into bars. Store loose in a plastic container at room temperature.

INGREDIENTS

1/2 cup **Butter**

1 1/2 cups **Graham cracker crumbs (just throw the graham crackers in a plastic bag and run the rolling pin over them and you'll have crumbs in no time!)**

1 1/3 cup **Flaked coconut**

Chopped nuts of your choice (or leave them out if nut allergies are a concern)

1 can **Sweetened condensed milk**

6 oz **Semi sweet chocolate chips**

Orange Anise Ring for Health, Happiness, and Prosperity

by J. C. DeCesari

DIRECTIONS

In a large bowl or in the bowl of a 5-quart stand mixer, add all the ingredients. Using a dough hook, mix the ingredients together into a uniform dough. It should form a nice, elastic ball. If you think the dough is too moist, add additional flour (a tablespoon at a time). The same is true if the dough is looking dry, add warm water (a tablespoon at a time).

Turn the dough out onto a floured surface and knead for about 15 minutes. Place in a greased bowl, turning it to grease all sides so that a crust doesn't form. Cover the bowl with plastic wrap and let rest for 10 to 15 minutes.

After resting, turn the dough bottom side up and press to flatten. Knead gently and proceed to create a ball. Place ball of dough onto a baking sheet lined with parchment, cover with plastic wrap and a warm damp dishtowel, and place in a warm spot to rise until it doubles in size.

Preheat oven to 400F.

Once the dough has risen, separate it into 3 smaller balls and roll them out into 20 inch strands. You want to make them long enough that they can be braided easily and then connect the ends to make a ring.

While you are preparing to braid the dough, focus on what you want to solidify in your life. Anise is used for protection and attracting good luck: oranges are great for prosperity, cleansing, and creativity: vanilla is a compelling herb, allowing you to assert your will over situations in your life.

Once you have braided the 3 cords, bring the ends around so that they meet and press them together, further solidifying your intention.

Place on a baking sheet and allow to bake for approximately 35 minutes, or until golden brown. Remove from heat and allow to cool.

This is an excellent recipe to enjoy during solar rites.

KCAL.	LEVEL
228	easy
approx. per serving	

SERVING	TIME
12-16	2
	hours

INGREDIENTS

1/2 cup	**Lukewarm water**
3/4 cup	**Freshly squeezed orange juice (4 medium oranges)**
2 tbsp	**Orange zest (always zest your oranges before squeezing them.)**
1 tbsp	**Extra-virgin olive oil**
1 tbsp	**Granulated sugar**
1 tsp	**Salt**
2 tbsp	**Dry milk**
1 tsp	**Anise seed**
1/4 tsp	**Anise extract**
1/8 tsp	**Vanilla extract**
3 cups	**Bread flour**
3 tsp	**Instant active dry yeast**

DIRECTIONS

Crust: Mix ingredients together, holding back ¾ cups of the mixture for the topping. Spread the rest in a greased, 9-inch, springform pan.

Filling: Mix the filling ingredients well and pour into the crumb lined pan. Sprinkle the remaining crumb mixture over the top.

Bake at 325F for one hour. Turn off the oven and leave the cake in the oven for another hour. Remove the rim of the springform pan, but not the bottom piece.

Modification – Just before serving, add fresh fruit like strawberries, blueberries, and raspberries on top, or heat some of your favorite jam in the microwave and drizzle on top.

INGREDIENTS

Prosperity Baked Cheesecake
by S. Connolly

CRUST

(1) 6 oz pkg	**Zwieback rusk toast finely crushed**
1 cup	**Sugar**
1 tsp	**Cinnamon**
1/2 cup	**Melted butter**

FILLING

4	**Eggs**
1 cup	**Sugar**
Pinch	**of salt**
	Juice of ½ a lemon
1/2 pint	**Sour cream (1 cup)**
1.5 lbs	**Cottage cheese (sieved fine)**
1/4 cup	**Flour.**

Shoe Fly Pie (Wet Bottom)

by M. A. Arguay-Wenner

INGREDIENTS

Two 10-inch pie shells, unbaked

3 cups	**Crumbs**
1 cup	**All-purpose flour**
1/2 cup	**Dark brown sugar**
	Butter, preferably unsalted, softened
	Optional: Add cinnamon and nutmeg to crumbs

	Filling
1 cup	**Molasses**
2 cups	**Dark brown sugar**
1	**Large egg**
2 cups	**Boiling water**
1 tbsp	**Baking soda**

Ancestry: Pennsylvania Dutch (Paternal)

Recipe: Shoofly Pie (Wet Bottom)

Main magical spices: Molasses, Cinnamon, Nutmeg, Brown Sugar

Practice: Braucherei (Pow Wow)

Intention: Healing

Deity: Jesus

DIRECTIONS

Shoofly Pie, a cherished specialty from Pennsylvania Dutch Country, is particularly beloved by the Moravian, Mennonite, and Amish communities. This regional treat holds a unique charm, steeped in history and tradition, and continues to resonate with those who savor its rich flavor and cultural significance.

Please note that this is a historical recipe collected and submitted by M. A. Arguay-Wenner. The recipe is from the 1800's and reflects the rich tradition of Pennsylvania Dutch folk magic. The intention for this pie is healing, so visualize healing energy flowing from your hands into the ingredients as you mix.

Preheat the oven to 350°F.

Mix the crumbs with your fingers (preferably) until it turns into fine crumbs.
Mix together molasses, brown sugar and egg with a whisk until smooth. Slowly add the baking soda to boiling water, stir until dissolved. Gradually add the water mixture to the molasses mixture and combine. Pour half of the liquid into each pie shell. Top each pie with equal portions of crumbs. Bake for about 40 minutes or until the top is dry. Place on baking rack and cool.

SERVING	*TIME*	*KCAL.*	*LEVEL*
16	60 *mins*	450 *approx. per serving*	*intermediate*

Lucifer's Fallen Angel Food Cake

by Jennifer Vatza

LEVEL *intermediate*

KCAL. **288** *approx. per serving*

TIME **60** *mins*

SERVING **8**

INGREDIENTS

Angel Food Cake From Scratch

1 cup + 2 tbsp	**White flour or cake flour**
1 3/4 cup	**White sugar**
1/2 cup	**Rose petals, powdered**
1 cup	**Hibiscus petals, ½ powdered and ½ dried petals**
12	**Egg whites**
1 1/2 tsp	**Vanilla extract**
1 1/2 tsp	**Cream of tartar**
1/4 tsp	**Salt**

Hibiscus Rose Simple Syrup

1 1/2 cup	**White sugar**
1 cup	**Water**
1/2 cup	**Rose water**
2 tbsp	**Hibiscus flowers**

CAKE DIRECTIONS FROM SCRATCH

Lucifer's Fallen Angel Food Cake makes a wonderful offering of devotion to Lucifer for all workings, spells, rituals, channeling, and demonolatry rites. Ever since I started working with Lucifer, I have associated roses with him and use them in offerings and ritual workings.

For this recipe, you can make the angel food cake from scratch or a premade store-bought Angel Food Cake Mix will suffice. There will be some differences in the recipe for both.

During the preparation process, regardless of preparing the angel food cake from scratch or using a store bought cake mix, you can set the mood for this ritual creation by invoking Lucifer and burning devotional incense or candles while reciting his Enn (Renich tasa uberaca biasa icar Lucifer) or listen to binaural beats or guided meditations on Lucifer (there are plenty on YouTube).

Preheat the oven to 325°F (163°C) with the oven rack placed in the lower middle section of the oven.

Use an angel food cake or bundt cake pan, ungreased.

Blend sugar using a food processor or blender so that it is powdery instead of granulated. Remove one cup of the sugar and set aside.

Grind rose petals and hibiscus petals into a fine powder. This can easily be done using a coffee grinder.

Combine the remaining sugar with the powdered roses/hibiscus, cake flour and salt. Blend well, then set aside.

In a large mixing bowl, (make sure to use the whisk attachment regardless of the mixer you're using) whisk the egg whites and cream of tartar on a lower medium speed until foamy (approximately one minute). Increase the speed to a high/medium and add the cup of sugar that was set aside. Whisk together until it's light and fluffy, then add the vanilla extract and whisk briefly.

Sift the flour mixture slowly into the egg white mixture. This should be done slowly and gently, folding it in with a rubber spatula so as to not end up with a densely deflated cake.

Pour the batter into an ungreased angel food cake pan or bundt cake pan. The cake will rise whilst it is baking.

Bake for 40-45 minutes at 325°F (163°C)

Remove cake from the oven and cool upside down on a wire rack or plate for 2-3 hours.

Set aside to cool whilst you prepare the Hibiscus Rose Simple Syrup topping

BOXED CAKE DIRECTIONS

In addition to one box of Angel Food Cake Mix, you'll need 1 and ⅓ cup water, 1 tbsp Rose Water (food grade), ½ cup rose petals (powdered), and 1 cup of hibiscus petals, ½ powdered and ½ dried petals.

As with the "from scratch method", set your intention.

Preheat the oven to 350°F (176°C) with the oven rack placed in the lower middle section.

Use an angel food cake pan or bundt cake pan, ungreased.

Steep water and rose water with a muslin bag containing hibiscus flowers. This will turn the water a crimson color. It will make the cake have a pink hue once it is finished.

In a large mixing bowl, using a hand mixer or a regular mixer, combine cake mix, water, rose water, powdered rose petals and hibiscus flowers. Beat on low speed for 30 seconds and then increase to medium speed for one minute.
Pour the batter into an ungreased angel food cake or bundt cake pan. The cake will rise whilst it is baking.

Bake for 37-47 minutes at 350°F (176°C) The top should be golden brown.

Remove from the oven and cool the cake upside down on a wire rack or plate for 2-3 hours.

SIMPLE SYRUP DIRECTIONS

Combine water and rose water and add a muslin tea bag with hibiscus flowers to color the water a crimson red. Let steep until desired color is achieved

Pour water and sugar into a saucepan and bring to a boil, stirring until the sugar is dissolved.
Allow to cool and pour into a mason jar or oil/vinegar decanter.

Refrigerate after it is complete.

FINISH/DECORATE CAKE

Using a basting brush, coat the visible surfaces of the cake with a thin coat of the Hibiscus Rose Simple Syrup.

Coat the top of the cake with Red Sugar or other cake toppings such as sprinkles, colored sugars, or confectioners sugar.

Garnish with fresh rose buds and enjoy!

Starters & Salads

Every feast begins with a spell of anticipation. Salads and starters set the table with enchantment, offering a taste of the magic to come.

New Start Pistachio Nut Salad
by S. Connolly

DIRECTIONS

Make this salad in the morning as the sun rises. Breathe in hope and new beginnings, and exhale anxiety, stress, and fear.

Mix all of the ingredients together while doing this breathing exercise until everything is mixed well. Refrigerate for at least two hours before serving

INGREDIENTS

2 **3.4 oz boxes of Pistachio Pudding Mix (you can use sugar free with this recipe)**

12 oz **Cottage cheese (consider lactose free for lactose intolerance)**

12 oz **Cool whip (or whipped cream if you prefer)**

8 oz **Crushed pineapple (fresh is fine, too. You can substitute grapes or banana here, too)**

1 cup **Mini marshmallows.**

1/2 cup **Pistachio nuts (optional)**

SERVING	TIME	KCAL.	LEVEL
20	60 *mins*	200 *approx. per serving*	*easy*

Whipped Cream
by S. Connolly

INGREDIENTS

1 cup **Heavy Cream**

2 tbsp **Sugar**

1/2 tsp **Vanilla Extract**

DIRECTIONS

In a cold bowl with a chilled whisk (or beaters), whip the mixture of the cream, sugar, and vanilla at a slow speed, increasing it to medium high. Continue until medium peaks form. If you overwhip, fold in more heavy cream.

Emotional Strength Spinach Balls
by S. Connolly

DIRECTIONS

Take a few moments to ground yourself at the kitchen counter. Cook the spinach and add 2 tsp of salt. Transfer it to a bowl where you will add the rest of the ingredients and mix. As you add each ingredient into the bowl, say aloud (or in your head if that makes you more comfortable), "I am strong, they are strong, we can overcome any challenge thrown at us."As you mix, draw a surge of emotional strength from the core of your being and visualize it flowing into the bowl.

Chill the bowl in the refrigerator for 15 minutes or up to an hour. Remove the mixture from the refrigerator and form it into balls. Bake on a baking sheet at 350F for 30-35 minutes. You can also freeze the balls for cooking later.

Other substitutions: You can use a box of Stove Top Stuffing in a pinch, in which case you would remove the 4 tsp salt, croutons, and the poultry seasoning.

INGREDIENTS

2	**9 oz packages of frozen chopped spinach or 18 oz of fresh chopped spinach.**
2 tsp	**Salt**
3	**Scallions, chopped**
6 oz	**Croutons from day old bread, cubed.**
4 tsp	**Salt**
3 tsp	**Poultry seasoning (store bought or you can make your own, see recipe below)**
6	**Eggs (you can use low fat egg alternatives like Egg Beaters)**
	Pepper and Garlic Powder to taste.

SERVING
2O

KCAL.
25
approx. per serving

TIME
1.5
hours

LEVEL
easy

Homemade Poultry Seasoning

2 tsp	**Ground dried sage**
1 1/2	**Ground dried thyme**
1 tsp	**Ground dried marjoram**
3/4 tsp	**Ground dried rosemary**
1/2 tsp	**Ground nutmeg**
1/2 tsp	**Finely ground black pepper**

Mix well and store in an airtight container.

DIRECTIONS

Get your deep fryer ready, or heat a skillet with olive oil - enough to fry the patties.

While mashing the hot parsnips, draw strength from your heart, out through your arms, through the masher and into the parsnips. Once mashed and with the parsnips still hot, continue focusing on courage and strength as you add the remaining ingredients and enough breadcrumbs to form patties.

You will need to eye the breadcrumbs. Add them tablespoon by tablespoon until you like the consistency. Form them into patties and deep fry or pan fry the patties in a skillet until brown. Serve plain or with some ranch dressing on the side

INGREDIENTS

1 cup	**Cooked and mashed parsnips**
1/2 cup	**Grated cheddar cheese**
1/4 - 1/2 cup	**Breadcrumbs (I like the Italian seasoned kind because they add more flavor)**
1 tsp	**Salt**
2	**Eggs**

SERVING	TIME	KCAL.	LEVEL
8	1.5 hours	85 approx. per serving	easy

Courage Parsnip Patties
by S. Connolly

Cool Down Tomato Salad

by S. Connolly

INGREDIENTS

6	**Roma tomatoes, cut in half and quartered with stems removed.**
4 oz	**Low moisture mozzarella cheese cut into cubes**
2	**Cucumbers peeled, halved lengthwise, seeds removed, and sliced**
1	**Medium red onion cut into bite sized pieces - about one inch.**
2 tbsp	**Balsamic vinegar**
4 tbsp	**Olive oil**
	Salt and Pepper to taste
	Italian seasoning blend spice mix (optional)

DIRECTIONS

While putting this together, visualize everyone being calm and collected and push that intent into the ingredients as you prepare them.

Stir together the tomatoes, cheese, onion and cucumber in a large bowl.

Add the vinegar, oil, salt, pepper, and the optional seasoning evenly over everything in the bowl. Toss lightly.

Serve immediately or chill to serve later.

SERVING	TIME	KCAL.	LEVEL
4	60 mins	255 approx. per serving	easy

SERVING	TIME	KCAL.	LEVEL
6	40 *mins*	93 *approx. per serving*	*easy*

Potent Pecker Parsnip Chips
by S. Amanda

DIRECTIONS

Invoke or call upon any spirits you choose to work with during this spell, if any. If practicing demonolatry, Asmoday is a great one for this because he is a daemon of physical strength, lust, and control of one's own mind. You can draw the daemon's sigil on the bottom of your baking sheet with solar charged salt water and or a drop of blood.

Preheat oven to 400F.

Thinly slice parsnip root either by hand or with a mandolin or vegetable slicer.

Place in a bowl and drizzle in olive oil, garlic, burdock root, solar charged sea salt, and black pepper. Mix well with your hands while focussing on masculine strength and sexual energy. I like to add in my energies and intentions as I'm mixing.

Place the parsnip chips onto a baking sheet in a single layer so as to not crowd them and place in the oven until crisp and golden brown on the edges(keep an eye on them as they can brown quickly). This spell keeps its potency even after consumption for up to 3 days. It will also gain potency the more often it's done so you can start doing the spell a few times a week and then taper it down to bi weekly as needed.

INGREDIENTS

4-6 **Parsnip roots(longevity, potency, masculine sexual energy)**

4 tbsp **Olive oil(healing, strength, protection)**

1 tbsp **Finely chopped fresh garlic(purification, lust, protection, immunity)**

1 tsp **Solar charged sea salt to taste (add the power of the sun and protection and blessings to your spell)**

1/2 tsp **Black pepper(protection)**

4 tsp **Burdock root finely chopped or powdered (only use 1 tbsp if using powdered since burdock root is a super potent aphrodisiac)**

In every simmering pot, a potion brews—rich with warmth, flavor, and a dash of magic. Soups and stews nourish both body and soul.

Rufus and Gruppenfuhrer's Anti-Lurgy Chicken Soup

by Rufus Vader

INGREDIENTS

3	**Large chicken breasts cut into bite size pieces or an equivalent amount of chicken leg meat.**
1	**Red onion**
1	**Shallot**
4	**Stalks of celery**
1	**Largish leek**
3	**Medium potatoes**
4	**Good size carrots**
1 cup	**Frozen peas or a tin of garden peas.**
1/2 a tub	**Double cream.**
	Salt
	Pepper
	Mixed herbs,
	A squirt of garlic purée.
1.5 liters	**Chicken/veg stock.**
	Chilis - see recipe.
	Flour
	Alcohol of your choice (to drink while making)

Make this recipe when the house is struck with colds, flus, or general "lurgy" type illnesses to help heal the body.

DIRECTIONS

In a large pan (I use a large wok), add about 2 ounces of butter and two dessert spoons of vegetable oil on medium heat. Add in the chopped chicken and gently cook.

While the chicken is cooking, start preparing the vegetables. First finely chop up the onion and the shallot and keep together. Chop up the rest of the vegetables into approximately 1cm cubes.

Once the chicken is fully cooked, remove from the pan and place in a separate bowl. Leave the juices/oil in the pan and add another 2oz of butter, the onions, and shallots. Cook on medium head for about 15-20 mins (do not burn). Once this is complete, add the rest of the vegetables to the pan and cook on medium heat. Add some mixed herbs, I add a tbsp of mixed herbs, a squirt of garlic purée, and some salt and pepper.

While this is cooking, think about the chili you will use. This will be down to how much heat you can take, and the severity of your Lurgy. The more severe the Lurgy, the more chili. I use two or three Thai Birdseye chili's, chopped. Add the chili and 2 tbsp of flour to the pan when all the vegetables are soft. Cook for five minutes.

Next, add the chicken stock and keep on a medium heat. Cook, covered, for 30-40 mins, stirring occasionally. Remove about 1/3 of the vegetables from the soup and then use a hand blender to blitz what is remaining. Once blitzed, add the removed vegetables, peas, and chicken that you set aside earlier. Replace the lid and cook for another 30 mins, stirring occasionally.

After 30 mins, taste and add salt/pepper if required. Once happy, stir in 1/2 a tub of double (thick) cream. Serve when you wish. Hint - let cool and rest for a few hours, reheat and then serve.

SERVING	TIME	KCAL.	LEVEL
6	1.5 hours	152 approx. per serving	easy

Warming/Healing Winter Stew

by S. Connolly

INGREDIENTS

1 lbs	**Beef stew meat cut into bite sized pieces**
4	**Large red potatoes peeled and cubed**
1	**Whole onion, chopped**
2	**Ribs of celery, chopped**
4	**Carrots, peeled and chopped**
1	**Parsnip, peeled and chopped**
1	**Rutabaga peeled and chopped**
2 qrts	**Beef broth (switch to chicken broth if you want to use chicken)**
	Garlic powder, salt, and pepper to taste

DIRECTIONS

If you need to heal the body and the mind, try this hearty winter beef stew.(You can also substitute chicken, pork, or turn it into a veggie stew.)

As you are chopping and preparing the vegetables and meat, visualize warmth and well-being. In a stockpot, add the broth. Next, add all the meat, vegetables, and spices. You can add additional spices as you wish. If you need more liquid, add water until all the ingredients in the pot are covered. Put the pot on medium heat and cover it, bringing it to a boil. Once it comes to a boil, turn the heat down and let it cook. I like to cook my stews for at least three hours, minimum. But I'll often start them around one in the afternoon and let them go until 6pm. It makes the house smell amazing. About a half hour before serving, taste the broth to see if it needs more salt or pepper, or additional seasonings you may wish to add. Once you get it to where you want it, let it cook another half hour so the additional spice has time to blend in.

Serve hot with a side of homemade bread and butter.

SERVING	TIME	KCAL.	LEVEL
6	4 hours	360 approx. per serving	easy

Dream Travel Chicken Soup With Yarrow And Mugwort

by S. Amanda

DIRECTIONS

Before adding any ingredients, write or paint, with solar charged sea salt water, the sigil of the spirit you choose to work with at the bottom of the pot. You should choose a spirit with whom you are familiar and have built a trusting relationship with, Your patron, or matron if you have one, would be awesome for this as well as a trusted ancestor. Invite them to join you while setting your intentions.

Place roughly chopped vegetables in the pot, then add the chicken and herbs. Bring to a boil and then down to a simmer.

Gently simmer for 4 hours or until the chicken is thoroughly cooked and beginning to fall off the bone.

Remove the chicken from the pot and set aside. Allow it to cool until safe to handle. Pull the meat from the bones and place back in the pot. If you used chicken breasts, give them a rough chop and place them back in the pot.

Simmer for another 20 minute. Serve warm.

This recipe freezes well so you can save some for a quiet evening when you want to focus on magical work and save your energies so you won't have to cook. This is perfect for rainy, autumn evenings, especially around Samhain which is a great time for dream travel and connecting with the astral. The veil is thinner during that time, however, any time of year it is great.

INGREDIENTS

1   Whole chicken or 4 chicken breasts
4   Stalks of celery roughly chopped
4   Carrots roughly chopped
1   Onion roughly chopped
6   Cloves garlic
3   Bay leaves
6   Sprigs of thyme
6   Sprigs of sage
3   Sprigs rosemary
    A handful of fresh mugwort or no more than 1 tbsp
    dried and ground
2   Stems fresh yarrow with flowers and leaves or 1 tbsp
    if dried and ground
    Solar charged sea salt

Main Dishes

The heart of any meal is its main dish, where magic and nourishment come together to create a feast worthy of celebration.

Luck of the Leaf Cabbage Rolls

by S. Amanda

DIRECTIONS

Belial is a great spirit to bring in for this dish. Light a candle and place it near the area you are cooking in. Green is my favorite color candle for this recipe. You can bless it with oil if you'd like. Invite the spirits to join you as you draw the sigil of the spirit in the bottom of a pot with solar charged sea salt dissolved in a little water. I write the sigil with my fingers as I believe this connects you to the food as well as the spirit. Feel free to put a little bit of bourbon aside for the spirit while you cook.

Simmer a head of cabbage in a pot of lightly salted solar salt water and start removing the leaves. Use a two-prong fork or tongs. Place the leaves on a pan after they cool. Snip the hard stem parts out with scissors and chop them up into the veggies.

For the filling, chop up the onions, carrots, celery, cloves, and garlic. In a separate dish, chop up the mushrooms and set aside. If you are cooking the vegetarian version, this is all you'll need for the filling.

Saute all of the vegetables, except the mushrooms, in a skillet until tender. This is best done with a little salt, pepper, and a couple tbsp of vegetable broth.

If you are using meat in this recipe, brown the meat in a separate skillet, then combine half the vegetable mixture.

Put the other half of the vegetables into a separate bowl. In the same skillet you used for the vegetables, add an oil of your choice (I use ghee), then add the chopped mushrooms, salt, pepper, and a couple spoonfuls of nutritional yeast. Saute the mushrooms until they have a little caramel color on them, then deglaze with a few tablespoons of vegetable broth. Add them into the bowl with the remaining half of the vegetables and set aside.

In the mixture of meat and vegetables, add 3 tablespoons of soy sauce and mix.

Spoon a bit of each mixture into the cabbage leaves and roll them up like a burrito. Drizzle oil over the rolls and sprinkle with salt if desired.

Roast in the oven at 400F for 40 minutes or until they have a good caramel color. Serve on top of rice.

Kindly thank your spirits for spending time with you and for assisting with your spell; let them know they can go when they are ready.

SERVING	TIME	KCAL.	LEVEL
5	2 hours	198	intermediate

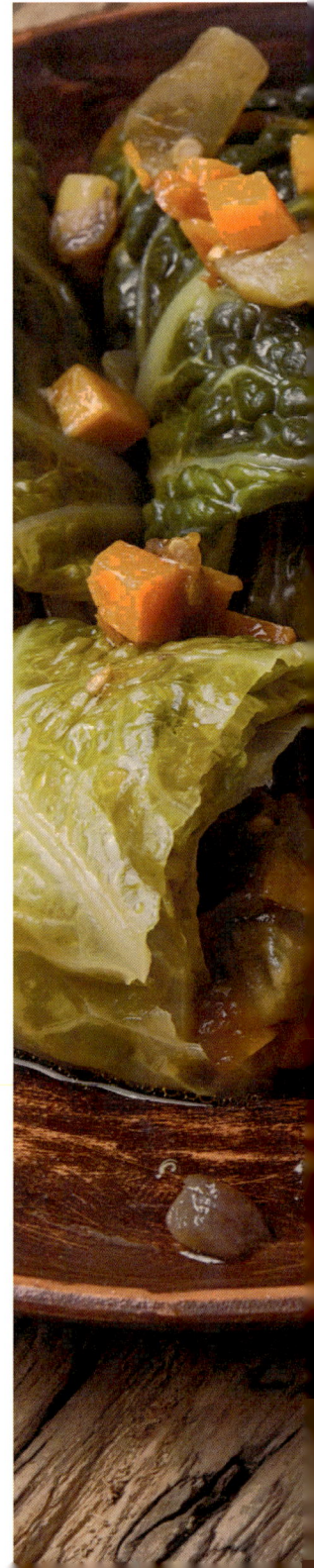

CABBAGE ROLL INGREDIENTS

1	**Head of cabbage**
6	**Carrots**
2	**Onions**
6	**Stalks of celery**
8	**Cloves of garlic**
1 inch	**Chunk of fresh ginger**
1/2 lbs	**Baby portobello mushrooms**
1 lbs	**Ground beef**
1 cup	**Vegetable broth**
4 cups	**Uncooked white or brown rice**
1/4 cup	**Nutritional yeast**

BOURBON SAUCE INGREDIENTS

1/2 cup	**Soy sauce**
1/4 cup	**Bourbon or apple juice**
1/2 cup	**Brown sugar**
2 tbsp	**Garlic chili oil**
1/2 cup	**Water**
6 tbsp	**Cornstarch**

BOURBON SAUCE DIRECTIONS

Let the cornstarch dissolve in the water while you simmer all other ingredients on the stove for approximately 10 minutes. Then add the cornstarch slurry and stir until clear and thickened. Drizzle the sauce over the rice/cabbage rolls before serving.

47

All-in-One Break, Block, Open, and Attract Authentic New Orleans Gumbo

by S. Amanda

SERVING	TIME	KCAL.	LEVEL
16	4	453	intermediate
	hours	approx. per serving	

INGREDIENTS

Oil of choice though, traditionally, I use lard or bacon grease.

1 lbs **Chicken (boneless thighs are best)**

1 lbs **Andouille sausage**

Shellfish (optional)

2 **Green bell peppers chopped**

6 **Stalks of celery**

2 **Large yellow onions chopped**

10 **Cloves garlic**

2 lbs **Okra, sliced about an inch thick (frozen is okay)**

2 tbsp **Filé (aka ground sassafras to help thicken the gumbo)**

1 cup **Flour**

6 **Sprigs of fresh thyme or 1 tbsp dried**

6 **Bay leaves**

2 tbsp **Tony's creole seasoning or a mix of paprika, cayenne pepper, onion powder, garlic powder, chili powder, and white pepper**

Solar charged sea salt to taste I sprinkle a little with each layer just a pinch and it seems to balance out perfectly.

12 cups **Chicken or vegetable stock**

4 cups **White rice**

1 **Lemon (chopped up - include rind but remove seeds)**

DIRECTIONS

Start by lighting a candle and invite your preferred spirit. I favor white candles and generally invite Satan to join me due to my belief that he brings everything together.

If you don't have a huge stock-pot, you can use a dutch oven, large saucepan, or multiple small pots and make in batches. Use your finger to write a sigil of your choosing on the bottom of your pot(s) to connect you with the spirit, ingredients, and energy of this dish.

Pour 1 cup of oil in the pot over medium-high heat. Add the chicken, brown well, then set aside in a separate dish. Next, add the Andouille Sausage to the pot, brown, then place in same dish as the chicken.

Do not rinse the pot. Add one cup of all purpose flour to the juices left behind. Stir often and watch carefully so as not to burn the mixture. You are going for what's called a "chocolate roux", simply put, browned. This process can take about 20-30 minutes. This is the perfect time to add in your intentions and connect yourself with the ingredients.

Once you have achieved a good chocolate/brown color, add the chopped onion, celery, and bell peppers. Stir occasionally until the veggies are cooked down and have become one with the chocolate roux. This takes about 20-30 minutes. Have patience and embrace the magic of what you are creating.

Next, add the garlic and lemon. Cook for another 5 to 10 minutes (enough to soften but not brown). Add the meats back into the pot, then add the herbs. Pour in the broth or stock into the pot. Stir well and bring to a boil.

Let simmer for an hour or longer (this is your preference - the longer you simmer, the longer the ingredients will have to "marry").

About 20 minutes before serving, speak your intentions into the filé and the okra then add them to the pot. Stir until thick and okra is cooked through but not too soft. You can invite your spirits and ancestors to join you in the meal if you'd like.

Cook the rice with 4 ½ cups water and 1//2 tbsp of solar charged sea salt.

Serve gumbo over the rice and add a little pile of filé on the side of your bowl to thicken as desired. Thank the spirits and let them know they may leave when they are ready though, I've known my spirits to stick around and enjoy the meal with me.

Money Monday Authentic Southern Cajun Red Beans and Rice

by S. Amanda

DIRECTIONS

Red beans and rice was historically cooked on Mondays in the deep south because Mondays were laundry/wash day and the women could let it simmer all day while they worked. In magic, Mondays are feminine and are associated with the moon, the element of water, and influenced by intuition, healing, and purifying. if you practice demonolatry, Azlyn is associated with Mondays and is great for asking questions about what may be in store, Belial is also great to help assist in manifestation and wealth.

Chop all of the vegetables to a medium size and then saute them in a skillet until they are a good caramel color. While you do this, set your intentions and add your energies. Breathe your magic into the food. The caramel color will add depth to the dish and to the magic you put into it.

Add in unsoaked beans (you can first rinse in salt water to purify, cleanse and protect if you want), then add in a bundle of thyme. Remember to speak your intentions with each ingredient.

Next, add the parsley and bay leaves. If you desire, write wishes, sigils, seals, desires, and intentions on the bay leaves with paint made of salt water before you add them.

Next, add in the smoked turkey legs (whole), 12 cups of chicken stock (you can do a mixture of stock/water), salt, hot sauces, and Worcestershire. Mix together.

Put a tilted lid on with a sigil underneath and bring to a rolling boil. This will get the energy moving quickly.

Reduce heat and simmer until the red beans are tender. I let mine simmer for several hours,

Remove the turkey legs and let cool before removing the meat from the bones (you can set the bones aside for future use in other spellwork or bury them in your yard to keep the energies near your home).

The gravy will be thin. Use a potato masher to mash up some of the beans.

Add the meat back into the pot and simmer until it is the consistency you want.

Serve on top of cooked rice. Freeze leftovers.

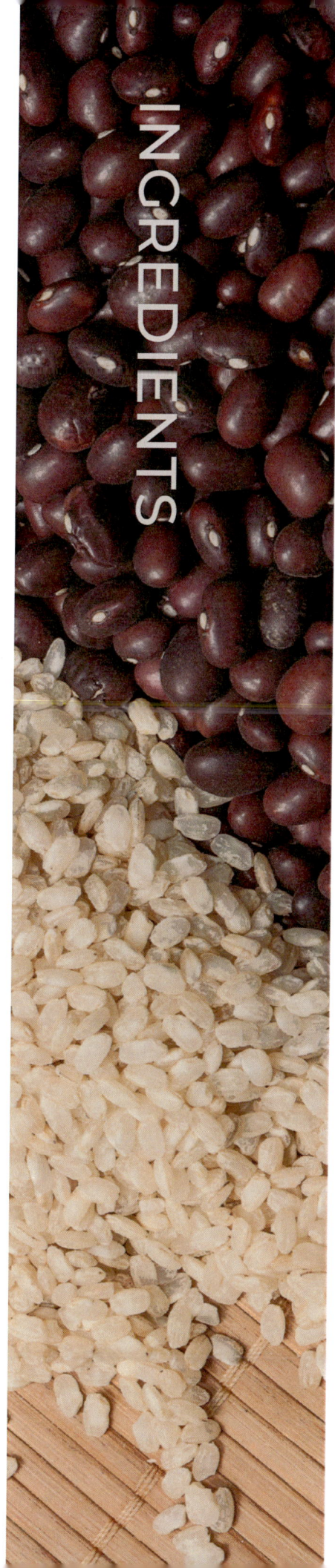

INGREDIENTS

1 **Groon boll popper**

1 **Red bell pepper**

4 **Stalks celery**

2 **Large yellow onions**

2 **Smoked turkey legs**

6 **Sprigs of fresh thyme to taste**

A handful of fresh parsley

6 **Bay leaves**

1 tbsp **Tony's creole seasoning or a mixture of red pepper, black pepper, salt, chili powder, onion powder**

1 tbsp **Paprika**

1 tbsp **Tabasco sauce and Louisiana hot sauce or hot sauce of choice**

1 tbsp **Worcestershire sauce**

Solar charged sea salt to taste though I recommend at least one good tablespoon during cooking then add more to taste later on

6 cups **Chicken stock (homemade bone broth is better)**

2 lbs **Dry Red beans, if you can't find true red beans, kidney beans will work**

4-6 **Unncooked rice**

Loving Kindness Lasagna
by S. Connolly

SERVING	TIME	KCAL.	LEVEL
12	2-3	400	intermediate
	hours	approx. per serving	

DIRECTIONS

This is a fantastic dish to make for a grieving family, new neighbors, or to take to a family or friend who needs a little pick me up. It's also a family favorite that goes over well with kids and adults alike. I grew up with an Italian grandmother who knew how to cook, and if anything gave us all a sense of love and well-being, it was grandma in the kitchen baking her lasagna that brought love and kindness to everyone who ever crossed its path.

First, assemble the sauce. In a high sided skillet, brown the ground Italian sausage until crumbly. Drain any excess fat. If you're using a high sided skillet, you can continue assembling the sauce in the same pan. Otherwise, transfer the cooked meat to the saucepan. Add to the cooked sausage the grated onion, the tomato paste and sauce, the sugar, the seasonings, and then salt and pepper. Bring the sauce to a boil, then lower the heat and bring to a simmer. Let it simmer until it cooks down and your sauce is thick. Adjust the seasonings to your personal taste.

In a large pot, add enough water so the lasagna noodles can float freely and have room to expand; add a dash of salt. Bring the water to a boil and then add the noodles. Boil the noodles until they're almost done, but not quite. They should be pliable enough to work with, but not so soft that they fall apart. Drain and let them cool. If you are adventurous and are making your own lasagna noodles from scratch, you can skip boiling them.

Next, make the cheese filling. In a bowl, mix the cottage cheese (or ricotta), 2 eggs, the parsley, and the salt and pepper. Mix until well incorporated and set aside.

Next, you will make the dry cheese blend by mixing the grated cheeses together in one bowl.

Lightly grease a 9 x 13 baking dish. Next, you will assemble the lasagna.

Place a layer of cooked noodles on the bottom of the pan. Then add a layer of the meat sauce. Then add a layer of the cheese filling. Then sprinkle some dry cheese over that. Add another layer of noodles, another layer of sauce, another layer of cheese filling, more shredded cheese, etc… Continue until you've run out of ingredients, or have filled the pan. Whichever comes first.

Bake in a 350F oven for 45 minutes to an hour. When you remove the lasagna, let it cool for 10 minutes before slicing it and serving it. This dish reheats well in the oven or microwave, and it freezes well, too. You can even prepare it ahead of time and keep it in the refrigerator, then let it come up to room temperature before popping it into the oven and baking it.

Modifications – feel free to add a few cloves of garlic to the sauce if you wish. Keep in mind the people you are making the dish for.

SAUCE INGREDIENTS

1 lbs	**Italian sausage (ground)**
1	**Medium onion – grated.**
1	**Large can of tomato paste**
1	**Small can of tomato paste**
1	**Can of tomato sauce or peeled tomatoes**
1/2 tsp	**Sugar**
2 tbsp	**Parsley flakes**
1 tbsp	**Italian spice mix (usually a variation including basil, marjoram, oregano, rosemary, and thyme – so you could mix your own in a pinch)**
	Salt and Pepper to taste.

CHEESE FILLING INGREDIENTS

1	**Large tub of small curd cottage cheese (you can use ricotta instead, but the original recipe calls for cottage cheese)**
2	**Eggs**
2 tbsp	**Parsley flakes**
	A little pinch of salt and pepper

Dry Cheese Blend Ingredients:

1	**6 oz block of scamorza cheese – shredded**
1	**6 oz block of parmesan cheese – grated**
1	**6 oz block of provolone cheese – grated**

PASTA INGREDIENTS

	Water
	Salt
1/2 lbs	**Lasagna Noodles (or half of a 1 pound box) for a 9 x 13 lasagna**

Motivation Pepper Steak

by S. Connolly

INGREDIENTS

1 cup	**Rice - cooked according to package**
1 3/4 cup	**Beef broth**
1 tbsp	**Soy sauce (light sodium is fine)**
1/4 tsp	**Garlic powder (or 1-2 cloves minced)**
1 lbs	**Beef steak, sliced thin (it's okay if it's not the greatest cut because you'll be cutting it thin)**
1	**Large green bell pepper sliced into strips**
1	**Medium onion cut into thin wedges**
3 tbsp	**Cornstarch**

DIRECTIONS

Make this pepper steak when you want to help give yourself or a loved one a motivational boost in the right direction. Peppers are great for enhancing energy and getting things moving forward.

Visualize lighting a fire under someone's rear as you stir the starch, broth, soy sauce, and garlic in a bowl and set it aside. Stir fry the beef in a wok or non-stick pan over medium heat until browned. Add peppers and onions, then stir in the starch and broth mixture. Cook until the mixture begins boiling, then turn down the heat and let it simmer until the sauce thickens. Add black pepper as needed. Serve over cooked rice.

SERVING	TIME	KCAL.	LEVEL
4	60 mins	330 approx. per serving	easy

SERVING	TIME	KCAL.	LEVEL
8	60	500	easy
	mins	approx. per serving	

Find Your Passion
Bacon Beet Burgers
by S. Connolly

DIRECTIONS

Beets bring out creativity and inspiration. This is the perfect dish to make when you or your loved ones are having a hard time finding their passion.

Your intention for this recipe is to inspire, so listen to inspiring music and think inspiring thoughts as you put this dish together.

Brown the meat, the onion and the beet. Add the soup, water, and bacon and simmer for 20 minutes.

Next, make the dough. Place it on a floured board and roll it out. Cut it into 4 x 6 strips. Add the mixture to one side of each dough piece, wrap it over, and press the seams with a fork. Place it on a baking sheet. Do this until you have used all your dough and meat mixture. Put a slit in each little pastry pocket to allow steam to vent.

Bake at 350F for 30-35 minutes or until the crust is golden brown. Let cool for 10 minutes, then serve.

You can substitute cabbage for beets and skip the soup if you want to turn these into lucky cabbage burgers!

INGREDIENTS

3 cups	**Flour**
1 cup	**Shortening (or butter)**
1 tsp	**Baking powder**
1 tsp	**Salt**
1 cup	**Milk.**
	Ingredients for filling:
6	**Strips Bacon – cooked crisped and broken up.**
1 lbs	**Hamburger**
1	**Large onion - chopped**
1	**Small beet – chopped**
2 tbsp	**Water**
1 cup	**Cream of mushroom soup (canned, not watered down!)**

Grandma C's Mood Enhancing Sweet & Sour Chicken (or Pork)

by S. Connolly

INGREDIENTS

1 cup **Rice (cooked according to the package)**

1 lbs **Chicken breast – cubed (or pork – cubed)**

1 **Carrot, chopped**

1 **Green pepper, chopped**

1 **Clove of minced garlic**

3 **Slices of pineapple – cubed**

2 tbsp **Soy sauce**

6 tbsp **Flour**

2 tsp **Cornstarch**

Olive oil

SWEET & SOUR SAUCE

5 tbsp **Vinegar**

5 tbsp **Catsup**

5 tbsp **Sugar**

4 tbsp **Pineapple juice**

1 tbsp **Soy sauce**

1 tbsp **Cornstarch**

5 tbsp **Cherry juice (or pineapple juice)**

1/2 cup **Water**

Cook until the sauce is thick and transparent.

DIRECTIONS

If your family or friends have entered your house unhappy, they'll leave with a smile on their face after having Grandma C's Mood Enhancing Sweet and Sour Chicken (or pork). Served over rice with a salad on the side, it's a perfect, quick and easy meal that's sure to please even the pickiest eaters.

In a bowl, add the meat, along with soy sauce, flour, and cornstarch - mix well, making sure the meat is well-coated. In a deep frying pan, add enough oil to fry the meat until it is brown. Drain. In another skillet, add 3 tablespoons of olive oil and add the clove of garlic, the carrots, the pepper, and the pineapple. Add the meat and cook for a few minutes. Serve over rice and drizzle with sweet & sour sauce.

SERVING	TIME	KCAL.	LEVEL
4	60 mins	560 approx. per serving	easy

Side Dishes

Side dishes may be small spells, but they bring harmony to every meal, adding color, flavor, and a touch of magic to the table.

Deep South Dirty Rice Dispel Spell
by S. Amanda

INGREDIENTS

1 cup	**Rice (cooked according to the package)**
1 lbs	**Ground beef**
1/2 lbs	**Andouille sausage**
2 tbsp	**Bacon grease**
1/4 cup	**Flour**
1	**Large yellow onion**
3	**Stalks celery**
5 cups	**Beef broth plus 2 separated**
1 tbsp	**Chili powder**
1 tbsp	**Oregano**
2 tbsp	**Parsley**
2 tbsp	**Thyme**
3	**Bay leaves**
3	**Garlic cloves, finely chopped**
1/2-1 tsp	**Cayenne pepper**
1 tsp	**Black pepper**
2 tsp	**Solar charged sea salt**
4 cups	**Rice, cooked**

DIRECTIONS

I prefer to start the rice in a separate pot before I start the rest of the dish. I use an instant pot to cook the rice in the beef broth.

In a large skillet, saute the ground beef and sausage. I prefer cast iron because it is great for protection, but a regular 10" skillet will do just fine.

Once the meats are browned, add in the bacon grease and flour (do not drain the grease from the meat). Cook approximately 5 minutes, being sure to coat each granular of flour in the grease to remove the raw flour tase.

Be sure to speak your magic into the dish as you cook.

Add in the bell pepper, onion, and celery. Saute until soft and translucent.

Add in the garlic and herbs. Allow them to soften slightly and omit their volatile oils into the mix (about 5 minutes). Then add the bay leaves (write protective sigils on them with solar salt water as your ink or your intentions before adding). If practicing demonolatry add daemon sigils of your choosing (Valefor is a good one for this, but I'd also recommend you add your matron or patron's sigil).

Add 2 cups of beef broth and stir until everything becomes a rich, gravy texture. Then add the already cooked rice. Mix everything together.

Add another protection and banishing sigil underneath a lid placed on top of the pot. Remove from heat and allow to marry well including your magic.

You can use this to protect all who eat in your home as well as send any enemies running. This recipe will help you recognize enemies in your midst and dispel any evil lurking around you.

SERVING	TIME	KCAL.	LEVEL
6	I	230	easy
	hour	approx. per serving	

Stewed In Love Southern Okra And Tomatoes

by S. Amanda

INGREDIENTS

1/2 lbs	**Bacon, cut into approximately 1 inch pieces**
1	**Large yellow onion**
6	**Cloves of fresh garlic, chopped**
1	**28 oz can of diced tomatoes, I like the fire roasted**
2-3 lbs	**Okra, sliced (fresh or frozen)**
3 cups	**Chicken stock**
1 tsp	**Solar charged sea salt**
1/2 tsp	**Black pepper ground**
1 tsp	**Tony's creole seasoning**

SERVING	TIME	KCAL.	LEVEL
6	40 _minutes_	257 _approx. per serving_	_easy_

DIRECTIONS

Using solar salt mixed with water you've blessed, draw a sigil of love (that you created), or the sigil of a demon of your choosing (Astorath and Furfur are good for this), on the bottom of a large skillet.

Fry the bacon pieces and remove once golden brown. Set aside.

Add in the chopped onion to the remaining bacon grease and saute until carmel in color. Add the garlic and cook for around 3 minutes.

Next, add the okra. Cook until slightly soft and no longer stringy in texture. Set your intentions while you stir in the can of tomatoes.

Slowly pour in the chicken stock and seasonings. Simmer without the lid for 30 minutes or until it's become thick like a stew.

This dish is perfect to eat by candlelight with your partner (red candle of course and if you want to dress your candle for extra intent, add sigils - this is a great addition to your spell). This goes great with pork roast.

SERVING	TIME	KCAL.	LEVEL
8	1.5 _hours_	212 _approx. per serving_	_easy_

DIRECTIONS

Wash the greens by soaking them in 1 tbsp apple cider vinegar and a tiny pinch of solar charged sea salt. Float in cold, clean water to cleanse for about 30 minutes. This will allow any residual sand or pests to sink. Remove and chop very roughly or tear with your hands. I prefer to use my hands as it's more personal, discarding any extra woody stem pieces. Set aside
.
In a large pot with a lid, cook the bacon, cut into pieces, until the fat has rendered and the bacon is slightly browned. Then remove the bacon from the pan and set aside.

Saute the onion in the bacon grease until it gets a slight carmel color to it. Add the chopped garlic and cook until soft and fragrant (say a money mantra while stirring if you'd like to add some oomph to it).

Add in the greens, ham hocks, bacon, and seasonings, along with the other tbsp of apple cider vinegar. Pour in the chicken stock or broth. Bring to a boil.

Stir a few times while adding in your intentions into the recipe, then lower the temperature. Simmer for about 45 minutes with the lid on. Sometimes, I will add a sigil under the pot lid to help things along. One that you've made yourself would be great for this and if you are a demonolatry practitioner, you can draw the daemons sigil of choice under the lid before you place it on. Belial is good for this recipe. You can also request assistance from any deity of your choosing or simply use your own energies.

Sprinkle a little vinegar (or pepper vinegar) over the spelled and prepared greens and enjoy.

INGREDIENTS

1 lbs	**Ham hocks or shanks**
1/2 lbs	**Bacon**
1	**Yellow onion**
6	**Cloves garlic**
3-4 cps	**Chicken broth or stock**
2 tbsp	**Apple cider vinegar**
	Tony's creole seasoning
	Solar charged sea salt
	Black pepper
2-3 lbs	**Collard greens**

Smooth Mind flow Southern Fried Okra

by S. Amanda

KCAL. **241** approx. per serving	LEVEL **intermediate**
SERVING **5**	TIME **60** mins

DIRECTIONS

Invoke the spirit of your choosing or call upon them to be present and assist with the spell. If practicing demonolatry, invoke or simply draw the daemon sigil of your choice. I prefer Volac in this recipe as he is really great for growth, as well as opening things and helping point you in the right direction when you are feeling stagnant. Draw the sigil of the spirit of your choosing on a piece of paper and dip it into the oil before you heat it. Set aside on a fire safe dish until you have prepared the rest of the dish.

Gently pat dry the okra with a tea towel or paper towel.

Mix the flour cornmeal and seasonings in a bowl. Set aside.

Pour the buttermilk in a separate bowl and set aside.

In a skillet, heat the oil to 350F (approximately 1 inch of oil).

Dip the okra in the buttermilk, then roll in the cornmeal. Fry several peaces in the preheated skillet (you can fry your lucky or magically significant number of okra to add depth to your spell). for approximately 3 minutes per side until they are golden brown. Remove from the oil and let drain on a paper towel or tea towel. Season with solar charged sea salt and pepper if desired. Repeat until all okra is fried.

Before consuming, burn the paper sigil on a fire safe dish over a bed of salt. Thank your spirits anytime you seek them for help.

INGREDIENTS

3 lbs	**Sliced okra, fresh or frozen**
1/2 cup	**Buttermilk**
1/2 cup	**All purpose flour**
1/2 cup	**Cornmeal, I prefer yellow**
	Solar charged sea salt to taste
	Black pepper to taste

Joyous Glazed Sweet Potatoes

by S. Connolly

INGREDIENTS

6	**Yams or sweet potatoes**
1 cup	**Orange juice**
1 cup	**Brown sugar**
1 cup	**Melted butter**

DIRECTIONS

I make these sweet potatoes during winter holidays and everyone loves them

As you assemble your ingredients, clear your mind of everything bothering you and concentrate on joy. Find joyful memories to focus on, or listen to music that brings you happiness.

Peal, cut in half, and then quarter the potatoes.

In a high sided skillet, on medium-high heat, add the orange juice, butter, and brown sugar. Mix until the sugar has melted.

Then add the sweet potatoes. Watch them carefully, spooning the mixture over the potatoes as they cook. The sauce will begin to simmer and as it cooks down and the sweet potatoes cook, the sauce will go from being thin, to a thick glaze. Be careful not to burn the potatoes by continuing to stir and turn them over as needed. The dish is done when a fork or knife easily penetrates and releases from the potatoes and the sauce has rendered down into that thick glaze. Approximately 15-20 minutes.

Pairs really well with ham, turkey, or Cornish hens.

SERVING	TIME	KCAL.	LEVEL
6	60 mins	540 approx. per serving	easy

SERVING	TIME	KCAL.	LEVEL
12	60 *mins*	240 *approx. per serving*	*easy*

Mom's Feel Good Potato Salad
by S. Connolly

DIRECTIONS

This side-dish is a family favorite for summer barbeques and will readily feed 10-12 people.

Remember that setting your intentions before you begin your recipe is key. Because this dish is often meant for social gatherings and having fun outdoors – you want to focus on good feelings and pleasant, even fun, social interaction. You can adjust your intent to warm wishes of health or prosperity too, to modify the spell for your particular need.

Start by hard boiling the eggs. Cool them down with cold water and ice, and de-shell them, giving them a quick rinse. Next, separate the yolks (in their own bowl) from the whites. Dice up the egg whites and put them in another bowl. Set these aside in the refrigerator for now.

Next, peel the potatoes and bring them to a boil in a large pan. Boil for one hour or until a fork slides easily in/out. Drain off the boiling water, give the potatoes a rinse with cold water, and then let them sit for 10 minutes to cool down. Once they're warm to the touch, cut the potatoes into bite sized pieces and add them to a large bowl. Set it aside.

Dice the onion and add to the bowl of potatoes. Take the egg whites from the fridge and add those as well.

Next, take the bowl with the yolks, and add the vinegar, mayonnaise, and mustard - mixing it together with a fork and crushing the yolks into the mixture until it's smooth. Using a spatula, add this creamy mixture to the bowl with the potatoes and mix carefully and thoroughly until the egg yolk, mayo, and mustard sauce covers all the potato, egg, and onion. Salt and pepper to taste.

You may need to add more mayo and mustard based on consistency and taste, too. You can serve it right away, or chill it in the refrigerator for a few hours. It refrigerates well, so you can make it the day before any potluck or gathering.

INGREDIENTS

5 lbs	**Red potatoes.**
12	**Eggs**
1	**White onion**
1/4 tsp	**White vinegar**
2 tbsp	**Mayonnaise (or Miracle Whip – mom always used miracle whip)**
1 tbsp	**Yellow mustard**
	Salt and Pepper to taste

From soothing teas to spirited brews, every sip carries a bit of magic, warming the heart and lifting the spirit.

Dreamwork Hot Toddy
by J. Priestly

INGREDIENTS

1 tbsp	**Dried hibiscus**
2 tsp	**Honey**
	Squeeze of lemon juice
	Splash of cognac or whiskey
	Splash of framboise

DIRECTIONS

Drink this tea if you wish an answer or secret be revealed to you in a dream or for any other dream work. The dried hibiscus aids in dreams, lucid dreams, divination and intuition. The raspberry from the framboise aids in dream magic and magical potency.

Steep dried hibiscus in a cup of hot water for about 7 minutes. Mix in honey, lemon juice, cognac/whiskey and framboise

While you mix the tea, envision the answer you are seeking being revealed to you or the intent of any dream work. Drink before sleep and you will know the answer by morning. You can also substitute the cognac/whiskey for calvados, the apple in the calvados aids in understanding and hidden knowledge.

Scrying Tea
by S. Connolly

INGREDIENTS

2 tbsp	**Mugwort**
1 tsp	**Cinnamon**
2	**Crushed cloves**
2 tbsp	**Chamomile**
2 tbsp	**Dehydrated apple slices**
1 tsp	**Ginger**

DIRECTIONS

Mix together, focusing on the third eye. Visualize the power centered there, infusing with the tea. You may say over it, "By Hecate may this tea increase the sight of anyone who drinks it." You can replace Hecate with any deity you wish, or leave that part out depending on your tradition. Once you have infused the tea with "the sight", store the tea in an airtight container. To brew one cup, add one heaping tablespoon of tea to a tea ball or tea strainer, cover with boiling water and let steep, covered, for 5-10 minutes. Makes approximately 8 cups of tea. Use before scrying rituals whether you're scrying with crystals, mirrors, water, or fire. This tea calms the mind, promotes focus, and opens the third eye.

Botis Tea of Reveal Malefica

by Jadean Lazulli

DIRECTIONS

This is a formula attributed to the Ars Goetia spirit, Botis, to reveal hidden malefica in readings when the user is hiding their magic.

Mix in equal parts and boil in an iron or steel pot, while reciting Botis enn (or invocation):

Jedan hoesta noc ra Botis. Ask for aid in seeing beyond the subterfuge. *Spirit of Water, Great President, Help me Reveal Malefica, reveal the harm that lurks in the astral plane hidden, may nothing remain occult.*

After drinking the tea you should be able to see malefica in your readings, that was hiding previously, if there was any.

INGREDIENTS

Lavender

Chamomile

Basil

Marjoram

Black Pepper

Tension Release Tea
(for relaxation and sleep)

by S. Connolly

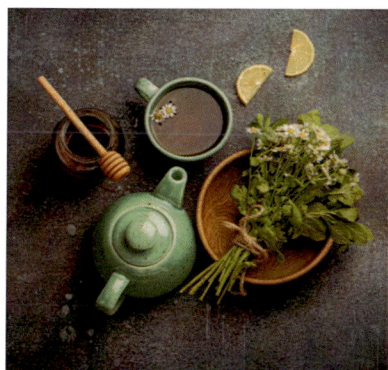

INGREDIENTS

1 tbsp **Ground up valerian root**

3 tbsp **Chamomile**

2 tsp **Lavender flowers**

1 tbsp **Passion flower**

1 tbsp **Lemon balm**

1 tbsp **Loose green tea (optional – it does have caffeine, but it also has agents to relax the mind.)**

DIRECTIONS

As you mix these ingredients together, visualize all the tension releasing from your muscles and relax your mind. Think only calm, relaxing thoughts. Store it in an airtight container. To brew one cup, add one heaping tablespoon of tea to a tea ball or tea strainer, cover with boiling water and let steep, covered, for 5-10 minutes. Makes approximately 6 cups of tea. I like to drink this tea an hour before bed while reading a book. I make the overall tea unflavored so I can add flavoring per cup based on my whim. To make this a single flavor tea – add a tablespoon of dried apple and ½ tsp cinnamon, or a tablespoon of chocolate pieces, or a tablespoon of mint to the overall tea.

DIRECTIONS

This is a lunar recipe meant to be drunk during ritual or individually or with a group, and has an included prayer at the end that you can say over the brewed mead before drinking/sharing it.

There are options here, depending on what you choose to use. Can boil water to purify and then steep herbs and fruit to make a tea.

Let mixture cool to 110F–115F before adding honey, stir until well mixed, remove cheesecloth full of steeping herbs or fruit, pour into 1st brewing bucket (the one with air latch in lid, add yeast and stir well. Seal bucket and allow to brew 3 months

When 1st brew is finished, strain into second bucket using a clean cheesecloth over lid of 2nd bucket brew another 3 months, tasting occasionally, handy spicket access. Strain again into clean/sterilized glass bottles, for storing, aging perfects it, enjoy!

Medicinal, devotional and recreational all at once, multipurpose nectar of The Gods

Magical Mead Prayer

We honor and call upon the energy of the Moon, Luna. Opening us to the awareness and possibilities of the hidden, unseen, deep within ourselves.

A triad of combined powers to create this Elixor. We honor the mysterious Bee nation, the power of the green, mighty plant nations and the life-giving water of our mutual Mother.

Allow us to hear our Soul words. Heal any dis-ease lurking in the shadows. Clarify and make us stronger, moving toward balance in all ways, individually and as a group.

Magical Mead
by Annette Archambeau

EQUIPMENT

- 2 - 5 gallon brewing buckets (1 that has a lid equipped with a bubble, air latch, the other bucket having a spicket installed near the bottom of the bucket) standard brewing buckets
- Sanitizing powder
- Large stainless-steel pot/ long armed wooden spoon
- Cheesecloth for herbs or berries added, and straining mead into containers.
- Tree tapping equipment if using maple or other tree sap.
- Glass bottles for the final product. Yields approximately 4 gallons.

INGREDIENTS

4 gals	**Purified water/distilled water/tree sap**
1-2	**Packets of champagne/wine yeast**
8 cups	**Locally sourced, raw honey**
2 cups	**Fruit or fresh herbs of your choice, wildcrafted and hand gathered is best (optional)**

Lilith's Infused Blood Honey
by Jennifer Vatza

INGREDIENTS

12 oz **Honey (any kind)**

1/2 tsp **Vanilla Paste**

20 **Drops of Datura Flower Essence (optional)**

8 oz **Dark Rum**

2 **Fresh Mandarin Oranges**

2-4oz **Hibiscus flowers**

1/2 oz **Peony Flowers**

1/2 oz **Blue Lotus Flowers**

1/2 oz **Poppy Flowers**

1 oz **Cinnamon Powder, Bark or Sticks**

1 oz **Clove Buds**

1 oz **Red or Pink Rose Petals**

Optional ingredients:

Datura tincture for a little extra kick.

A few drops of your own blood, using a diabetic lancet, for ritual use and only used by yourself for safety against blood borne pathogens.

Substitutions:

Agave nectar or Simple Syrup in place of honey for a vegan version.

Water or other types of alcohol can be used in place of Rum, such as bourbon, whiskey, and flavored liquors or bitters would work well.

Vanilla beans or extract can be used in place of vanilla paste. Beans would need to be cut for the infusion.

DIRECTIONS

Lilith's Infused Blood Honey is a sultry infused honey that can be used for ritual purposes as offerings or to connect with Lilith. The formulation is based upon correspondences with Lilith. It can also be used to flavor teas, tinctures, and other beverages or as a topping on fruits, yogurts, or other desserts. The concept and formulation came via a surprise channeling session with Lilith.

You can set the mood for this ritual creation by invoking Lilith and burning devotional incense or candles while reciting her Enn (*Renich viasa avage Lilith lirach*) or listen to binaural beats or guided meditations on Lilith (there are plenty on YouTube).

Pour 12 ounces of honey into a crock pot or double boiler on low heat for 6-8 hours.

Add the juice from two fresh squeezed mandarin oranges into the honey and stir.

Add the Datura flower essence or other optional ingredients and blend well.

In a separate bowl, combine 3 ounces of Hibiscus Flowers with 8 ounces of Dark Rum and let sit while preparing the rest of the recipe. The hibiscus flowers will turn the rum a dark crimson red over time. This will add the blood red color to the infused honey.

Combine remaining hibiscus flowers, peonies, poppies, blue lotus, rose petals, cloves, cinnamon bark (if using sticks they can directly be added to the honey) You may have some left over afterwards.

Grind the herbal mixture so it blends well. A small coffee grinder will do the trick or a mortar and pestle.

Add the blended herbs to the honey infusion and stir well.

Strain the hibiscus from the rum and add to the honey infusion and still well. This will help the honey to be more pliable.

After 6-8 hours strain the honey infusion. You can use a strainer to do this keeping in mind that you may have to strain it a few times to remove most of the herbal particulates. You may have to use some pressure to separate the honey from the herbs. It may take awhile to fully strain the honey.

After complete, add to a mason jar or ritual container. I prefer vintage glass decanters or oil and vinegar bottles. You can add Lilith's sigil to the outside of the jar or bottle. The final yield may vary depending on how well the honey strains from the herbal infusion.

Ritually consecrate the honey infusion. You can do a middle pillar rite or simply charge it on your Lilith altar.

Check out the resources section at the back of the book for where to buy the ingredients in this recipe.

Shae's Divination Tea

By J. C. DeCesari

DIRECTIONS

You can adjust the amounts of everything to suit you. This usually makes about a half a gallon of tea. I put it in the fridge and enjoy it either hot or cold.

Fill a saucepan with water and add all ingredients.

(You can also add lavender, ginger, jasmine flowers, catnip, chamomile, or rosehips)

Once it has hit boiling, turn it down and leave it to simmer on low for 15 minutes or so.

Strain and add your sweetener of choice and then enjoy.

I also like to add some lemon juice as well and when I feel that I might need more kick I will add some wormwood tincture to it as well.

INGREDIENTS

4-6	**Black tea bags**
4 or 5 tbsp	**Hibiscus flowers**
1 tsp	**Lemon balm**
1-3 tbsp	**Mugwort**
1-2 tbsp	**Wormwood**
1-2 tsp	**Cinnamon**
1-2 tsp	**Cloves**
1-3 tsp	**Nutmeg**
	Several star anise

Magical Properties of Ingredients

Pantry Staples

Baking Powder/Soda: Energy, magic, personal power.

Beans: Wisdom, divination, prosperity, and abundance.

Beer: Dreams, purification, offerings, and insight.

Bread: Each type of bread has its own properties, so it depends on the grain used. That said, all breads are good for offerings and grounding.

Butter: Peace, spirituality, and connection to nature.

Cake: Happiness, rituals, rites of passage, offerings, celebrations, grounding, and attraction. Through ingredients, cakes can also be made for any purpose under the sun.

Cheese: Success, happiness, good news, and lucky windfalls.

Chocolate: Prosperity, positive energy, happiness, love, and attraction.

Coconut: Protection, purification, and healing.

Coffee: Energy, clarity, divination, and focus.

Curry: Energy, passion, desire, and momentum.

Gravy: This can depend on the type of gravy. Overall though, gravy calms and heals the emotions and can cleanse and purify the soul.

Honey: Use for healing or binding (due to stickiness), or for relief of allergies (use local honey).

Ice Cream: This can vary depending on the flavors you add, though ice cream can promote spiritual love toward others and promote community.

Jelly: Many say jelly promotes happiness, but this can vary based on the flavor or fruits in the jelly.

Maple Syrup: Can draw or attract love, money, or energy, it can be used for healing, but it can also be used to bind someone or something.

Milk: Because milk feeds babies, it is often associated with feminine power, goddess energy, moon magic, nurturing, love, and spirituality. It's often used for cleansing and offerings as well.

Olive Oil: This is often the base oil used for ritual oils. It rules over spirituality, integrity, passion, fertility, healing, peace, protection, and luck. It is also said to magnify magical power.

Pasta: Is said to enhance psychic powers, provide protection, and to boost communication and creativity.

Peanut/Peanut Butter: Rules over masculine energy, and brings prosperity. It can also be used in health magic for those who may suffer from any wasting diseases.

Soy Beans: They rule over fertility, passion, prosperity, luck, psychic powers, and spirituality. A very versatile bean.

Sugar: Promotes both love and protection.

Tea: Helps with meditation, intuition and insight, and can promote courage, strength, and prosperity.

Vanilla: Use in recipes for love, spiritual growth, sex magic, passion, and creativity.

Vinegar: Often associated with fire energy. Promotes cleansing, purification, protection, and transformation.

Wine: Often used as an offering to the spirits. But it is also added to meals or dishes to bring happiness and love.

Yogurt: Can enhance creativity and help heal depression. Add various fruits to adjust the magical properties slightly. Because yogurt is a dairy product, it can also bring comfort, love, and nurturing into the recipe.

Vegatables and Legumes

Acorn Squash: Used for protection, adaptation, power, and longevity.

Asparagus: Use in dishes to enhance fertility, cleanse the emotions, and to draw passion or lust. Serve asparagus before any working of sex magic.

Avocado: It has long been associated with fertility and virility because of its shape. Encourage men to eat it to increase stamina in and out of the bedroom. It also contains healthy fats, so include it in healing dishes.

Beans: They bring abundance, luck, and new beginnings.

Beets: Use beets for dishes to enhance passion, beauty, love, and virility. Beets can also be used to strengthen friendship or feelings of love between family and friends. Because of the color, you can use beet juice in place of blood inks or as a substitute for blood magic.

Broccoli: Add this veggie to any dish to promote protection, prosperity, luck, and peace.

Butternut Squash: Often used in healing recipes, especially stews and soups. Probably due to how nutritious and rich in vitamins and antioxidants they are. They can also help regulate blood sugar.

Cabbage: This is a very versatile vegetable that promotes protection, abundance, and luck. You can make magical inks from the purple variety to use in spells for prosperity and protection.

Carrot: This root vegetable is ruled by Mars. Because of its shape, it is associated with lust and fertility. When eaten by women, it is believed it encourages pregnancy. Because they come in various colors – white, orange, and even purple, you can choose your carrots based on the color of your intention. The flowers of wild carrots are called Queen Anne's Lace. However, do not pick and eat wild carrots unless you know for sure what you are doing as wild carrots can closely resemble poison Hemlock which, if ingested, can be deadly.

Cauliflower: Is said to boost power during magical workings, especially those of divination. It can also be eaten as a symbol of self-purification before ritual work.

Eggplant: Used for protection and to ward evil and negativity.

Garlic: Often associated with protection, garlic is used to ward off evil, revoke enemies, and exorcize negative spirits. It can be burnt to fumigate a space of all negative energy and astral sludge as well. It is also believed to heal sickness, so add it to soups and other dishes for healing.

Lettuce: This plant is ruled by the water element because it's made up mostly of water. Ruled by the moon, it was eaten to prevent sea-sickness. It can also be utilized in protection dishes. It is said if you plant it in your garden, it will protect your home. Lettuce was rubbed on the face and forehead to help insomnia. It was also used in divination.

Onion: (also leeks and scallions) Considered a masculine root, this plant is used in various forms of magic. It was thought that when you cut an onion open and leave it in a room, it will absorb any sickness. Adding it to healing stews and dishes will help the body heal. It is believed that if you grow it in your garden, it will protect your home against evil spirits. It is also thought to produce prophetic dreams, and attract money as well as lusty partners.

Peas: Are said to draw compassion, money, love, and connection with family, friends, and community.

Peppers: Spicy peppers can add some spice and hot energy to magical dishes. Spicy peppers can also be used to cause harm, to protect from enemies, and to send enemies away.

Sweeter peppers also provide protection. They can also bring in money, and wisdom, and be used in magic that deals in matters of love.

Potato: Once thought to be poisonous, as they're part of the nightshade family, they are now a very common food all over the world. Ruled by the moon, potatoes can be used in healing magic. They can also settle a sour stomach.

Pumpkin: This squash provides protection and can ward off friends and foe who are predatory. Pumpkin repels evil spirits and draws protection and comfort into the home. It can also be used to protect and boost finances.

Radish: Can repel negativity and be used in protection recipes. Some lust dishes also include radish.

Tomato: This is a fruit, but most people still view it as a vegetable. It is considered a powerful aphrodisiac, but can also promote friendship and community.

Turnip: Used for banishing and cleansing, include them in recipes for protection and to destroy negative situations and obstacles. Turnips have also been used in fertility magic.

Zucchini: Again, because of the shape, zucchini are often used in sex magic, or magic to keep your partner faithful. It can also be used in protection and prosperity.

Fruits

Apple: Used in love, healing, and divination recipes. Like all fruits, apples can be left as offerings in temples.

Banana: Protection against accidents and to increase sexual potency. Used in lust magic due to its shape.

Substitutions

Allspice = 1tsp = 1/2 tsp cinnamon, 1/4 tsp ginger, and 1/4 tsp cloves

Apple Cider Vinegar - White Vinegar

Beer or Wine - broth (beef or chicken - some say better with chicken) or apple cider vinegar. Alternatively you can use non-alcoholic beer, or non-alcoholic cider.

Baking Powder - 1/4 tsp baking soda and 1/2 tsp cream of tartar for every 1 tsp baking powder.

BBQ Sauce - Ketchup and a few drops of liquid smoke.

Bread Crumbs - Cracker crumbs or ground oats. You can also toast bread and then grind it up in the food processor.

Broth, Chicken or Beef - 1 chicken or beef bouillon cube and 1 cup of boiling water per cup of broth. Note that bouillon comes in cubes, or as loose powder. A lot of people feel the loose powder dissolves more readily.

Brown Sugar - Sugar with Molasses. Example: 1 cup brown sugar = 1 cup sugar and 2 tbsp molasses.

Butter - 1 cup butter = 1 cup margarine or 1 cup shortening with 1/2 tsp salt.

Buttermilk - Powdered buttermilk. Or for every cup of buttermilk use 1 cup of milk and 1 tbsp vinegar.

Cheddar Cheese - substitute with colby cheddar or Monterey Jack

Chocolate - 1 oz unsweetened chocolate = 3 tbsp unsweetened cocoa powder plus 1 tbsp vegetable oil

Cornstarch - for every 1 tbsp - 2tbsp all purpose flour or arrowroot powder

Corn Syrup - substitute the same amount with honey or sugar. If using sugar, add 1/4 cup of liquid for each cup of sugar.

Cream of Tartar - same amount of white vinegar or lemon juice.

Dried Herbs (vs. Fresh) - Use 1/2 tsp dried herbs in place of every 1 tbsp fresh

Eggs - 3 tbsp of mayonnaise per egg.

Evaporated Milk - Same amount of light cream.

Fish Sauce - 1 tbsp = 1 tbsp soy sauce + minced anchovy

Flour (self rising) - For each cup add 1/2 tsp salt and 1.5 tsp baking powder

Garlic - 1/8 tsp garlic powder for every clove of fresh garlic

Heavy Whipping Cream or Half & Half - 1 cup of milk and 2 tbsp of melted butter.

Honey - Use 1 1/4 cup white sugar in 1/3 cup water or use 1 cup corn syrup or 1 cup light treacle syrup

Lemon Juice - for every teaspoon, use 1/2 tsp vinegar and 1 tsp lime juice

Mayonnaise - Use either sour cream or yogurt in the same amount called for.

Milk - Use soy milk, rice milk, almond milk, cashew milk, or use 1/4 cup powdered milk to 1 cup of water

Oil - Applesauce

Oil - Margarine or Butter

Onion - 1 tbsp dried onion (with water added to reconstitute them) = 1 small onion. Conversely, if a recipe calls for onion powder but you want to use fresh onion, use one medium onion in place of 1 tablespoon of powdered onion.

Red Pepper Flakes - 1/2 tsp red pepper flakes = 1/4 tsp cayenne pepper or hot sauce like Franks Redhot or your choice.

Shortening - Cooking oil in the same amount called for. Use 1 and 1/8th cups of unsalted butter for 1 cup of shortening. If using salted butter in your recipe, decrease any added salt by 1/2 tsp.

Sour Cream - Use one cup of Greek Yogurt, or mix 1 tbsp vinegar or lemon juice and add to a cup of milk to make one cup of sour cream. (Only works for recipes where you're baking or cooking with sour cream - not for garnish.)

Sugar (white granulated) 1.5 cups of corn syrup, or 1 cup of brown or powdered sugar for every cup of regular sugar. You might also consider Sucralose (Splenda) which you can also substitute cup for cup.

Tomato Sauce - Use equal parts of tomato paste and water until you reach the amount you need. You can add fresh or canned tomatoes for additional flavor and will need to add spices to taste.

Vanilla Extract - use the same amount of maple syrup, brandy, rum, or bourbon.

Yogurt - buttermilk, sour cream, or cottage cheese (cup for cup)

Glossary of Terms

Bake - to cook food by dry heat without direct exposure to a flame, typically in an oven or on a hot surface.

Blanch - to briefly immerse food in boiling water, especially as a technique for removing the skin from nuts or fruit or for preparing vegetables for further cooking.

Boil - to cook by immersing a food in boiling water or stock.

Braise - to fry food lightly and then stew it slowly in a closed container.

Fry - to cook food in hot fat or oil, typically in a shallow pan, but also in a deep fryer.

Grill - a metal framework used for cooking food over an open fire; a gridiron.

Parboil - to partly cook food by boiling

Poach - to cook by simmering in a small amount of liquid.

Roast - to cook food, especially meat, by prolonged exposure to heat in an oven or over a fire.

Saute - to fry quickly in a little hot fat.

Simmer - (of water or food) to stay just below the boiling point while being heated.

Measurements

Imperial measurement abbreviations
tablespoon (tbsp) = tablespoon
teaspoon (tsp) = teaspoon
fl.oz = fluid ounce
oz = ounce
c = cup
pt = pint
qt - quart
gal - gallon
ml = milliliter
lb = pound
F = Fahrenheit
C = Celsius

Metric measurement abbreviations
g = gram
kg = kilogram
ml = milliliter
l = liter

Other cooking abbreviations
hr = hour (s)
min = minute (s)
doz = dozen

Basic cooking measurements conversion chart
Dash = less than ⅛ teaspoon
1 teaspoon = ⅓ tablespoon = 5 ml
1 tablespoon = ½ fluid ounce = 15 ml
1 fluid ounce = ⅛ cup = 30 ml
¼ cup = 2 fluid ounces = 4 tablespoons = 59 ml
⅓ cup = 2.7 fluid ounces = 5 tablespoons and 1 teaspoon = 79 ml
½ cup = 4 fluid ounces = 8 tablespoons =118 ml
⅔ cup = 5.3 fluid ounces = 10 tablespoons and 2 teaspoons = 158 ml
¾ cup = 6 fluid ounces = 12 tablespoons = 177 ml
1 cup = 8 fluid ounces = 16 tablespoons = ½ pint = 237 ml
2 cups = 16 fluid ounces = 32 tablespoons = 1 pint = 475 ml
4 cups = 32 fluid ounces = 2 pints = 1 quart = 946 ml
2 pints = 1 quart
4 quarts = 1 gallon = 3.8 L

Cooking and Baking at High Altitude

Keep in mind two key factors when cooking at a high altitude: time and temperature. As elevation increases, the atmospheric pressure decreases, or becomes thinner. The atmosphere becomes drier, and liquids evaporate more rapidly, resulting in the need for changes in cooking methods. High altitude is defined as an elevation of 3,000 feet or more above sea level. Even at elevations of 2,000 feet, the temperature of boiling water changes from the standard 212°F at sea level to 208°F.

Boiling or simmering foods at high altitude means lower temperatures and longer cooking times. That said, with baking it is okay to experiment and just use the regular oven temperature for a shorter period of time but be sure to watch it so you don't overcook or undercook your food. I generally bake cookies, bread, and muffins at the temp called for in the recipe and cut 3-5 minutes off the baking time. Ensure your food is cooked long enough yet stays moist and full of flavor with these four tips.

Add a Quarter
Moist heating methods for meat and poultry, such as boiling, simmering or braising, will take up to 25% more cooking time. For example, if you are simmering a roast at 325°F that would usually take two hours to cook at sea level, that same roast cooked at high altitudes at 325°F would require 2 ½ hours of cooking time. Increasing cook time does not apply to oven-roasted meat or poultry; oven temperatures remain unaffected in high altitudes. Use sea-level cooking instructions for oven baking.

Increase Cook Time, Not Heat
Hiking up the temperature while boiling foods will not cook food faster. The liquid will simply boil away more quickly, and food will dry out. The temperature of a boiling liquid cannot exceed its own boiling point, except when using a pressure cooker. Instead, increase the cook time.

Cover Your Food
Retain moisture in meat and poultry products or any boiled food by tightly covering the pan during cooking. To continue to keep foods moist, cover dishes after cooking.

Use a Food Thermometer
To avoid undercooking or overcooking meat, poultry and leftovers, especially in a high-altitude environment, use a food thermometer to confirm internal temperature.

Meat Temperature Chart

Poultry 165°F (75°C)
Poultry, ground 165°F (75°C)
Beef, ground 160°F (70°C)
Beef, steak or roast 145°F (65°C)
Veal 145°F (65°C)
Lamb, ground 160°F (70°C)
Lamb, chops 145°F (65°C)
Mutton 145°F (65°C)
Pork 145°F (65°C)
Ham 145°F (65°C)
Ham, precooked and reheated 165°F (75°C)
Venison, ground 160°F (70°C)
Venison, steak or roast 145°F (65°C)
Rabbit 160°F (70°C)
Bison, ground 160°F (70°C)
Bison, steak or roast 145°F (65°C)

Acknowledgements

From S. Amanda: I am extremely thankful for so many people and the amazing amount of support that I've gotten in this. My dream of writing a cookbook started at a very young age. I have always had a passion for cooking and kitchen witchery but it was something I had put aside in my adult years and had regretted it, but as they say you can never start too late. I would like to thank Stephanie who is an amazing witch demonolatress and dear friend as well as a complete wealth of knowledge and community in one person thank you for showing me that my knowledge is important to others and encouraging me in so many ways I would not have taken this leap without her support and encouragement as well as her giving me the utmost respect and allowing me to be myself. I want to thank my dear Appalachian friend and witch Stacy for helping me find my strengths and showing me that my knowledge is worth sharing and for being there to support me in every way possible, thank you for being such a bootiful inspiration to me! Lastly I want to thank my family especially my husband Greg and my amazing children for being understanding of my weirdness and giving me the time needed to accomplish my dreams while simultaneously and unapologetically allowing me to be myself no matter how weird I am, he has embraced me through all of it and I'm forever thankful for him. I also want to thank everyone who has pushed me to share my knowledge. Thank you dearly and I truly love you all. ~ S. Amanda

About The Authors

S. Connolly has been studying and practicing all things magic and occult since 1984. She has over 50 books published on the topics of Daemonolatry and Daemonolatry magic, as well as general witchcraft and demonology. She grew up cooking and baking with her mother and grandmother and has always melded the magical with the culinary.

S. Amanda is a practitioner of demonolatry as well as southern conjure and is a self-taught herbalist. She has always had a passion for cooking and utilizing ingredients to bring connection with people and each other. She has roots in the deep south and embraces her French Cajun and Creole heritage while residing in the Colorado Rocky Mountain area. She is an artist, entrepreneur, and small business owner who has her hands in a little bit of everything from oils and incense to natural healing and body care. She is into wild foraging and herbal potion making for healing, wool felting, and taxidermy. Also a bone artist, she has been a medium since childhood and embraces spirit communication. One of her main goals in life is to help others see that through dark times comes beauty and growth, and to understand that sometimes not everything uncomfortable is something terrifying or evil.

Contributors

Annette Archambeau has a deep connection and love for the natural world. An alternative healer, focusing on nutrition, wild plant magic and energy. Co-founder of Archway Adventures
www.archwayadventures.org

M. A. Arguay-Wenner has a bachelor's degree in Political Science from the University of Albany and a master's degree in Spiritual Studies from St. Bernard's College of Theology. She is a professional photographer and writer.

J. C. DeCesari Ph.D. is the high priestess of The House of Delepitoré. A funerary priest, and teacher of magic, she has been practicing and working with the Daemonic Divine since the early 1980's. She wrote Meditations with the Death Daemonic, and co-authored Four Daemon Queens and Foundational Correspondences for Daemonolaters with S. Connolly.

Jadean Lazulli is a Demonolater, animator, artist and general misfit. He is an occult practitioner with 15 years of experience from Mexico. He wishes to offer a special thanks to Bearny A. Borunda.

Nathair Noxumbra is a practitioner of Traditionalist Witchcraft/Sinisterism/Afro-Caribbean Spirituality. He has been a practitioner for 59 years and is a elder in the Witch/LHP Community.

J. Priestly is a theistic Satanist and Demonolater who has always had a passion for cooking and baking since he was a child. In recent years, he has started incorporating magic into his cooking. So far, most of his recipes are targeted around prosperity, protection, and emotions. He is currently working on recipes for execration purposes.

Rufus Vader - From the UK. he started his journey in the 1980s when he obtained a copy of The Necronomicon by Simon. He then found Tezrian's Vault in the late 90s (when he managed to work out how to use the internet at university) and is honored to own number 48 of (100 published) Stephanie Connolly's Modern Demonolatry from 1999. The rest is history. He is a Mathematician/Statistician/Physicist. He would like a motorcycle but the missus says he can't have one. He has three rescue cats, Luna, Zuul and Annie.

Jennifer Vatza Is a practicing Occultist and Demonolatress, Reiki Master, Crystal Healer, Certified Aromatherapist, herbalist, perfumer, and skincare formulator. She brings her education in the arts into her experience in occult practices, energy work and healing into her product creation and occult content for her YouTube Channel and her business, Belladonna's Botanicals.

Resources

Hoodoo Food: The Best of the Conjure Cook-Off and Rootwork Recipe Round-Up Presented by the Ladies Auxiliary of Missionary Independent Spiritual Church (Missionary Independent Spiritual Church, 2014)

The Kitchen Witch by Sky Alexander (Simon and Schuster, 2023)

Most herbs can be found at *Penn Herb Company*, *Starwest Botanicals*, *Mountain Rose Herbs*, *High Wind Farms*.

Datura Tinctures and Flower Essences: *The Jagged Path*, *The Poisoner's Apothecary*, and *Bane Folk*.

Blue Lotus flowers can be found at *Schmerbals Herbals*.

Poppy and Peony flowers can be found at *Herbal Mansion*.

www.ingramcontent.com/pod-product-compliance
Lightning Source LLC
Chambersburg PA
CBRC091801090426
42811CB00021B/1905